► Community Reparation for Young Offenders

DOI: 10.1057/9781137400468.0001

Other Palgrave Pivot titles

David F. Tennant and Marlon R. Tracey: **Sovereign Debt and Credit Rating Bias**

Jefferson Walker: **King Returns to Washington: Explorations of Memory, Rhetoric, and Politics in the Martin Luther King, Jr. National Memorial**

Giovanni Barone Adesi and Nicola Carcano: **Modern Multi-Factor Analysis of Bond Portfolios: Critical Implications for Hedging and Investing**

Rilka Dragneva and Kataryna Wolczuk: **Ukraine between the EU and Russia: The Integration Challenge**

Viola Fabbrini, Massimo Guidolin and Manuela Pedio: **The Transmission Channels of Financial Shocks to Stock, Bond, and Asset-Backed Markets: An Empirical Analysis**

Timothy Wood: **Detainee Abuse During Op TELIC: 'A Few Rotten Apples'?**

Lars Klüver, Rasmus Øjvind Nielsen and Marie Louise Jørgensen (editors): **Policy-Oriented Technology Assessment Across Europe: Expanding Capacities**

Rebecca E. Lyons and Samantha J. Rayner (editors): **The Academic Book of the Future**

Ben Clements: **Surveying Christian Beliefs and Religious Debates in Post-War Britain**

Robert A. Stebbins: **Leisure and the Motive to Volunteer: Theories of Serious, Casual, and Project-Based Leisure**

Dietrich Orlow: **Socialist Reformers and the Collapse of the German Democratic Republic**

Gwendolyn Audrey Foster: **Disruptive Feminisms: Raced, Gendered, and Classed Bodies in Film**

Catherine A. Lugg: **US Public Schools and the Politics of Queer Erasure**

Olli Pyyhtinen: **More-than-Human Sociology: A New Sociological Imagination**

Jane Hemsley-Brown and Izhar Oplatka: **Higher Education Consumer Choice**

Arthur Asa Berger: **Gizmos or: The Electronic Imperative: How Digital Devices have Transformed American Character and Culture**

Antoine Vauchez: **Democratizing Europe**

Cassie Smith-Christmas: **Family Language Policy: Maintaining an Endangered Language in the Home**

Liam Magee: **Interwoven Cities**

Alan Bainbridge: **On Becoming an Education Professional: A Psychosocial Exploration of Developing an Education Professional Practice**

DOI: 10.1057/9781137400468.0001

palgrave▸pivot

Community Reparation for Young Offenders: Perceptions, Policy and Practice

Nicholas Pamment
University of Portsmouth, UK

palgrave
macmillan

DOI: 10.1057/9781137400468.0001

First published 2016 by
PALGRAVE MACMILLAN

The author has asserted his right to be identified as the author of this work
in accordance with the Copyright, Designs and Patents Act 1988.

Palgrave Macmillan in the UK is an imprint of Macmillan Publishers Limited,
registered in England, company number 785998, of Houndmills, Basingstoke,
Hampshire, RG21 6XS.

Palgrave Macmillan in the US is a division of Nature America, Inc.,
One New York Plaza, Suite 4500 New York, NY 10004-1562.

Palgrave Macmillan is the global academic imprint of the above companies
and has companies and representatives throughout the world.

Hardback ISBN: 978-1-137-40045-1
E-PUB ISBN: 978-1-137-40047-5
E-PDF ISBN: 978-1-137-40046-8
DOI: 10.1057/9781137400468

Distribution in the UK, Europe and the rest of the world is by Palgrave
Macmillan®, a division of Macmillan Publishers Limited, registered in England,
company number 785998, of Houndmills, Basingstoke, Hampshire RG21 6XS.

Library of Congress Cataloging-in-Publication Data is available from the
Library of Congress

A catalog record for this book is available from the Library of Congress

A catalogue record for the book is available from the British Library

For my parents

DOI: 10.1057/9781137400468.0001

Contents

List of Figures   vii

List of Tables   viii

Foreword   x
Lord Carlile of Berriew CBE QC

1 Introduction   1

2 Reintegration to Retribution:
   The Development of Unpaid Work for
   Offenders in England and Wales   7

3 Realising the Potential: The Research
   Evidence Base for Unpaid Work   29

4 Youth Justice Community Reparation
   in Practice   56

5 Conclusion: The Future Direction of Youth
   Justice Community Reparation   75

Bibliography   83

Index   103

DOI: 10.1057/9781137400468.0001

List of Figures

4.1	Age of participants	57
4.2	Referral point	57
4.3	Offence leading to referral	58
5.1	Summary of evidenced-based principles for the delivery of unpaid work most likely to lead to successful outcomes	77

List of Tables

2.1 1998 sentencing framework   15

2.2 Current sentencing framework   19

3.1 Comparison of 'raw' adult reconviction figures 1983–2003 (*Custody, Probation, Probation with 4A/4B requirements* and *Community Service*)   31

3.2 Offender characteristics within the four disposal groups   33

3.3 Two-year reconviction rates for community penalties and custody   33

3.4 A comparison of offender characteristics by disposal (males only)   34

3.5 Actual and predicted reconviction rates by disposal (criminal history and social variables)   35

3.6 Adult reconviction: results from the 2001 Cohort   36

3.7 Community orders detail: reconviction rates by requirement type, 2009 Cohort (requirements selected here are based on 100 or more offenders)   36

3.8 Summary of studies into adult community service   38

3.9 Offenders' attitudes and contact with beneficiaries (acquisition of skills and usefulness of work)   41

3.10 Views on community service as a sentence, by order type   43

3.11 Views on community service impact   44

3.12 Reconviction rates by community disposal for males in 2001   47

DOI: 10.1057/9781137400468.0003

3.13   Summary of studies into youth justice community
       reparation   48
3.14   Reconviction rate by type of restorative intervention
       (34 projects)   51
3.15   Summary and integration of positive and negative practices
       relating to unpaid work (YJCR and adult CS) most likely to
       lead to successful outcomes   53
4.1   Placement type by non-skills and skills-based activities   59
4.2   Offenders' qualitative responses to the acquisition of skills 61
4.3   Offenders' qualitative responses to 'problem solving'   64

DOI: 10.1057/9781137400468.0003

Foreword

This timely publication is the first to make a really profound, fully researched examination of community reparation for young offenders. It is timely, given the reduction over recent years in the number of young offenders in custody, and the apparent appetite of the present Secretary of State for Justice to increase the long-term effectiveness of sentencing.

The notion of reparation has developed in recent years. Seen at first as a form of recognition of the real effect of crime on victims, its scope has broadened as practitioners have witnessed the important and beneficial effect on offenders' own perception of their actions when they become part of restorative justice activities. There is now no doubting the combined effect of reparation in (i) making victims feel better about the insult done to them, and (ii) making offenders behave better in the future through an enhanced understanding of the consequences of their actions. This book lays out a clear analysis of those processes, and leaves the reader with a strong notion that community reparation, properly applied, must be recognised as one of the most effective sentencing options available. It demands dedication, imagination and hard work on the part of service providers, and commitment on the part of the offenders, but it is clear that in many cases those combined aims can be fulfilled.

The cost benefit of effective community reparation is beyond doubt. The successful reintegration of unhappy and disaffected young men and women into the flow of everyday normality promises a reduction in the later use

DOI: 10.1057/9781137400468.0004

of adult prison sentences, cohesive family life, and increased respect between generations.

The value of the extensive and methodologically rigorous research undertaken by Nicholas Pamment enables us to evaluate the type of work undertaken as part of reparation. He demonstrates that the merely menial is likely to prove less productive and successful than programmes which challenge thinking skills. A critical faculty is not a privilege provided only to those with higher education. Young people have a profound moral sense, indeed often moral 'codes' shared with their friends and peer group. Sometimes those values can be distorted and even dissipated in self-justification, or blaming others for a sense of separation from parents or other legitimate authority. Community reparation can counter those failures, by fostering in former offenders their own critical faculty as to what really is right or wrong, what they would regard as reasonable if done to them. This is an important discussion, and the book stimulates it by its reliance on real evidence, founded on the experience of participants.

I believe that future practice will be influenced by this book, which should become required reading for practitioners, including lawyers and judges at all levels.

Lord Carlile of Berriew CBE QC

DOI: 10.1057/9781137400468.0004

palgrave▶**pivot**

1
Introduction

Abstract: *Community reparation for young offenders involves unpaid work such as painting and decorating, graffiti removal and shrub clearance. Often described as the juvenile version of adult community service, the disposal is available for offenders aged 10–17 and it remains a major part of the youth justice landscape within England and Wales. This chapter begins by defining the notion of 'reparation', before outlining the central argument of the book. The chapter then goes on to summarise the overall methodological approach, providing a justification for the primary research methods utilised within this study. It concludes by providing a concise overview of the proceeding chapter structure.*

Pamment, Nicholas. *Community Reparation for Young Offenders: Perceptions, Policy and Practice.* Basingstoke: Palgrave Macmillan, 2016. DOI: 10.1057/9781137400468.0005.

Defining community reparation

Reparation has been defined as '*any action taken by the offender to repair the harm s/he has caused*' (Wilcox and Hoyle, 2004, p. 17). There are two types of reparation. 'Direct' reparation occurs when an offender has some level of contact with the victim and this can be through a letter of apology, face-to-face meeting or practical activity. Alternatively, community reparation, which is the focus of this book, involves unpaid work for the general benefit of the local community, such as painting and decorating, litter picking and graffiti removal (Wilcox and Hoyle, 2004; YJB, 2000, 2008; Sumner, 2006; Pamment and Ellis, 2010). This work *could* be undertaken during evenings or weekends over a period of three months, and it could involve local statutory, voluntary, faith and business partners, as well as private individuals (YJB, 2008).

In 2010, community reparation was rebranded and promoted to the public under the banner of '*making good*' (YJB, 2010). However, this is suggestive only of restoration to the victims, conveying very little of what positive involvement may mean for the offender. Certainly, the notion is conceptually anomalous, with clear tensions between reparation which is re-integrative and reparation which is punitive (see Zedner, 1994; Sumner, 2006). By its definition, reparation must be a constructive process, whereby there is a lasting change in the attitude of the offender. As Braithwaite and Pettit (1990, p. 61) acknowledge, achieving such change may entail the offender undertaking practical training, facilitating social reintegration.

This book argues that youth justice community reparation (YJCR) has the potential to be a highly successful re-integrative intervention for young offenders. Indeed, the research evidence base presented in Chapter 3 shows that offenders *should* be provided with a variety of 'meaningful' work placements, which facilitate the acquisition of employability skills, essential for reintegration and desistance from crime (McGuire, 1995; Hollin and Palmer, 2006). Activities *should* also involve problem solving and challenge, motivating the offender and encouraging positive behavioural change, associated with reductions in re-offending. Additionally, the work *should* maximise contact with beneficiaries and placements must be perceived by offenders as worthwhile and useful to the community, increasing the sense of reparation (McIvor, 1991, 1992). It is important to note, however, that the evidence base surrounding unpaid work for offenders is not extensive and there is a lack of high quality research within this field.

DOI: 10.1057/9781137400468.0005

Why research community reparation?

There are few notable studies which have explored adult offenders on community service and these are now somewhat dated (Varah, 1981; McIvor, 1991, 1993; Rex *et al.*, 2003). Most importantly for this study, there has been no research explicitly focusing upon community reparation for young offenders. Instead, there have been two national evaluations of wider ranging youth justice sanctions, which have only briefly examined community reparation, resulting in limited and descriptive analyses (Holdaway *et al.*, 2001; Wilcox and Hoyle, 2004).

Nevertheless, these evaluations have highlighted the poor quality of workplace provision and the deteriorating performance of YJCR. Whilst undertaking an evaluation into [then] new strategies that addressed youth offending behaviour, Holdaway *et al.* (2001, p. 101) discovered that offenders were being allocated to a very limited range of unskilled tasks, consisting primarily of 'unchallenging' shrub clearance work. Furthermore, there was little correlation between the tasks, offender and offence. This resulted in a number of staff within one Youth Offending Team (YOT) believing that community reparation was merely a '*junior form of* [adult] *community' service with minimal reparative benefits'*. It was concluded that community reparation was deteriorating into a '*tokenistic response'*, whereby offenders gain very little from the process (Holdaway *et al.*, 2001, p. 38).

As part of a national evaluation of restorative justice interventions undertaken three years later, Wilcox and Hoyle (2004) briefly examined YJCR. Again, the results were described as '*unfavourable'* as offenders were being allocated to a limited range of menial activities, which were primarily perceived as a punishment and of no value to victims or the wider community. It was concluded that community reparation was not functioning as intended and not developing the interests or skills of young people.

We are therefore left with a dilemma. Whilst the disposal remains popular with sentencers, limited research has cast doubt upon whether the delivery of community reparation matches the evidence base of what is thought to be effective. Certainly, there is evidence of poor quality workplace provision, where some YOTs are providing a 'formulaic response' with little consideration for the young offenders and the attainment of employability skills. Arguably, this is reflected in the increasingly high reconviction rates over time following Reparation Order

DOI: 10.1057/9781137400468.0005

intervention, rising from 54.2% in 2002 to 67.2% in 2009 (Ministry of Justice, 2011a, p. 24), prompting the necessity for this study.

Despite such evidence of worsening effectiveness, there is no doubt that the YJB places significant emphasis on community reparation as a successful sanction, remaining a core component of the Youth Crime Action Plan (YJB, 2008). It is argued that community reparation reduces offending, benefits the community, provides reassurances as to the young person's future offending behaviour and is suitable for all levels of intervention, including high risk offenders subject to Intensive Supervision and Surveillance (ISS) (YJB, 2010).

In this period of austerity, consecutive governments have also seen unpaid work as a method of achieving overall resource savings, advocating new rehabilitation providers, greater use, increased hours and most importantly, more 'robust' conditions (Ministry of Justice, 2012b; Solomon and Silvestri, 2008; YJB, 2009c; YJB, 2008). However, as this book argues, if 'robust' is used as a euphemism for 'tough', there is nothing new in this and the disposal will fail. If robust means 'effective' and 'evidenced-based' there is every indication that YJCR will succeed and make a substantial contribution to reductions in prison costs and the failure of earlier 'tough' alternatives like the ISSP (Ellis, Pamment and Lewis, 2009). Thus, this research is of immediate relevance to youth justice policy.

Research approach

This study, therefore, critically evaluates young offenders' perceptions on the extent to which YJCR delivery in England and Wales matches the evidence base of what is thought to be effective. In order to achieve this, the text aims to: (1) Examine the comparative historical, political and legislative development of both adult CS and YJCR; (2) Review and integrate the research evidence base for adult CS and YJCR; (3) Evaluate YJCR in practice within a single YOT 'case study' area, utilising primary research to examine the perceptions of young offenders and their supervisors, drawing upon both secondary case file data and the previously identified evaluation evidence base; and finally, (4) Provide a critique of the organisation and delivery of YJCR.

Through a triangulated or combined methodology (see Bryman, 2008), this study utilised three primary data collection methods throughout the three year research period. As a community reparation supervisor, the bedrock of the study was in-depth participant observation, working alongside the young people during work placements, building rapport and encouraging a work ethic, thus becoming a 'member' of the observed group (Robson, 2002, p. 314; Jupp, 1989, p. 57; DeWalt and DeWalt, 1998). The key themes and findings from the literature review and observations were then utilised to compile assisted questionnaires for the young offenders.

Reflecting previous negative experience of interviewing severe and persistent offenders (see Holt and Pamment, 2011), assisted questionnaires were utilised with 97 young people. These provided a focal point for participants' attention, facilitating a 'visual aid to interface' between researcher and respondents. Within the questionnaires, a 'mixed methods' summated rating or Likert scale data collection instrument was utilised, originally developed as a way of measuring psychological attitudes (see Likert, 1932; Gay, 1996).

In total, there were 14 simple statements, whereby participants responded with a numerical indication regarding their strength of feeling towards the assertion. This study utilised the optimum seven-point scale (Miller, 1956), where 1 represents a low negative opinion and 7 a highly positive agreement. These responses were then entered into SPSS[1] and an Independent-Samples *t*-test was carried out to investigate any statistically significant differences between those offenders given skills-based and those given non skills-based work placements (Brace, Kemp and Snelgar, 2009). However, unlike 'purely' positivist scales, participants' responses were used to facilitate discussion and the generation of much qualitative data.

The assisted questionnaires for young offenders were then utilised to form the basis of a semi-structured interview schedule with 12 supervising staff. The overall benefit of this mode of delivery was to ensure consistency and gain responses to specific topics that could be analysed and compared to those of offenders. It also facilitated in-depth discussion and the production of qualitative data from busy YOT workers, who advocated such an approach (Nee, 2004; Noakes and Wincup, 2004).

Following primary data collection, the YOT provided case file information relating to every young person within this study. Key components included age; offence type (leading to referral); type of order (referral point); community reparation hours undertaken; breach information and *ASSET* scores.[2] After obtaining these cases, the data was coded and then analysed by the researcher using SPSS. Although access to the

YOTs database was restricted and dependent upon the co-operation of administrative staff, this final phase of the study formed an integral part of the overall 'combined' research strategy. Having provided an outline of the methodological approach, the following section provides a brief overview of the structure of this book.

Book overview

Chapter 2 provides, uniquely in England and Wales, a holistic and systematic critique of the historical, political and legislative development of both adult CS and YJCR. It demonstrates how successive legislative changes and the political requirement for increased visibility have placed a more substantial emphasis on the retributive power of the disposals. It concludes by stressing the need to rediscover the rehabilitative and re-integrative benefits of getting offenders to undertake unpaid work. Drawing upon national reconviction data and relevant studies, **Chapter 3** reviews and integrates the research evidence base for unpaid work. It argues that there is a paucity of high quality research into community reparation for young offenders. **Chapter 4** presents the results of the primary research study, integrating the findings from both the quantitative and qualitative methods used. Following an analysis of YOT case file data, key themes covered include participants' perceptions of skills acquisition; problem solving; punishment; benefits for the community; reparation and attitudes towards offending. The chapter uncovers serious inadequacies and failings regarding the organisation and delivery of community reparation for young offenders. **Chapter 5** discusses the main conclusions of the research and it presents established principles for the successful delivery of unpaid work for offenders. It highlights major implications for future practice and identifies important areas for further research.

Notes

1 Statistical Package of the Social Sciences.
2 Introduced in April 2000, *ASSET* is a structured assessment tool used by YOTs in England and Wales, in order to assess young offenders' needs and risks of re-offending (Baker, Jones, Roberts and Merrington, 2002; Gray, 2005; for a critical appraisal, see Baker, 2004).

DOI: 10.1057/9781137400468.0005

2

Reintegration to Retribution: The Development of Unpaid Work for Offenders in England and Wales

▶ **Abstract:** *This chapter provides a critique of the historical, political and legislative development of both adult community service (CS) and youth justice community reparation (YJCR). It outlines the development of the Community Service Order (CSO) for adult offenders, charting its transformation from a re-integrative alternative to custody in 1972, to punishment in the community through the Criminal Justice Act 1991. It goes on to discuss the major implications of the burgeoning popular punitiveness that developed in relation to young offenders in the early 1990s; the introduction by New Labour of the Crime and Disorder Act (1998) and most importantly, the introduction of community reparation for young offenders. It concludes by stressing the need to rediscover the rehabilitative benefits of getting offenders to undertake unpaid work.*

Pamment, Nicholas. *Community Reparation for Young Offenders: Perceptions, Policy and Practice.* Basingstoke: Palgrave Macmillan, 2016. DOI: 10.1057/9781137400468.0006.

A Re-Integrative Alternative to Custody: Adult Community Service (1972–1991)

Offenders undertaking work in the community is not new. Lasor, Hubbard and Bush (1996) for example, argue that the idea of 'reparation' can be found in the Old Testament and, from the 16th century, the English Houses of Corrections used hard work as a way of addressing laziness (Pease, 1980; Melossi and Pavarini, 1981; Reddy, 1991). However, as others have done (see Reddy, 1991), this chapter will chart the immediate legislative development of adult CS in the modern era, from the 1960s. With regards to criminal justice, this was an important period in the UK. There was then, as there is now, a growing concern about the increasing prison population, its high cost and apparent ineffectiveness (Maruna, 2001, p. 7). Furthermore, there was an emergent realisation that incarceration was damaging to individual offenders and their families, an awareness that continues up to the present day (Home Office, 1969; Bergman, 1975; Bottoms, 1987; Hine and Thomas, 1996; Worrall, 1997; Her Majesty's Inspectorate of Prisons for England and Wales, 1997; Travis, 2007; Clarke, 2011).

A subcommittee of the Advisory Council on the Penal System, chaired by Baroness Wootton of Abinger, was tasked with the development of alternatives to custodial sentences. In their final report: '*Non-custodial and Semi-custodial Penalties*' (Advisory Council on the Penal System, 1970), they proposed Community Service Orders (CSOs) for adult offenders. Pease (1985, p. 1) later defined the CSO as a '*penal sanction in which convicted offenders are placed in unpaid positions with non-profit or governmental agencies*'. According to Worrall (1997, p. 92), CSOs were the most helpful and imaginative of all the committee's recommendations.

The Advisory Council argued that CS was not only cheaper than incarceration (see McIvor, 1993), but could also fulfil several sentencing aims (Mair, 1997; Pease, 1985, p. 57). First and foremost, it would involve punishment, as offenders would be deprived of their liberty whilst they attended compulsory work placements, later termed a 'fine on time' (Worrall, 1997, p. 91). However, the committee hoped that offenders would not come to see the sanction as '*wholly negative or punitive*' and it stressed that constructive activity could contribute to a changed outlook on the part of the offender (Advisory Council on the Penal System, 1970 par 34; McIvor, 1993; Ellis, Hedderman and Mortimer, 1996; Hine and Thomas, 1996).

DOI: 10.1057/9781137400468.0006

The Advisory Council also advocated that the CSO would restore offenders' self dignity and esteem as they would be completing work for the benefit of the community (Advisory Council on the Penal System, 1970, p. 13). Crucially, unemployed offenders were expected to gain skills and a work ethic, thus combating social isolation and improving their communities' negative perception (see also Cartledge, 1986; Knapp, Robertson and McIvor, 1992; McIvor, 1992; 2010; Reddy, 1991; Walgrave, 1999; Rex *et al.*, 2003). Moreover, this could be achieved whilst offenders retained employment and family support, which custodial sentences could destroy (Petersilia, 2005; Tonry and Petersilia, 1999; Murray and Farrington, 2005). It is fundamental to note here, as others have done (Rex and Gelsthorpe, 2002, pp. 311–312), that the re-integrative emphasis and skills base placed on the CSO was considerable right from its inception, as evidenced by the Advisory Council's suggestion that offenders could work in conjunction with non-offenders (see also Bergman, 1975; Duguid, 1982; Hine and Thomas, 1996; Gelsthorpe and Rex, 2004; McIvor, 2010).

Following the recommendation by the Advisory Council, the CSO was introduced by the Criminal Justice Act 1972 and it was initially piloted in six probation areas (Pease *et al.*, 1975), before national implementation in 1975.[1] The CSO involved offenders aged 16 or over,[2] undertaking between 40 and 240 hours of unpaid work for the community and probation officers were charged with work allocation and general oversight regarding offender compliance, though direct supervision was by sessional supervisors (see Pease *et al.*, 1975, p. 2).

The CSO displayed immense potential, especially as an alternative to incarceration (Advisory Council on the Penal System, 1970; Pease *et al.*, 1975; NAPO, 2010). Indeed, the British experience quickly became the most studied (Pease, 1985, pp. 51–55), serving as a model that attracted interest from other European countries.[3] Similar schemes were thus introduced in Switzerland (1974), Germany (1975) and Italy and the Netherlands (1981) (for a global overview see: Harris and Lo, 2002; see also: Young, 1979; Pease, 1985; Hudson and Galaway, 1990; McIvor, 1992; 1993; Worrall, 1997; Killias, Aebi and Ribeaud, 2000).

CS in England and Wales was eagerly embraced by sentencers and 30,830 orders were imposed in 1982 (McIvor, 1993, p. 385; Hine and Thomas, 1996). However, during early pilot studies, CS was only replacing custody in approximately 45% of cases, thus not reducing the prison population at the level anticipated (Pease *et al.*, 1977, p. 9; see also Pease

DOI: 10.1057/9781137400468.0006

et al., 1975; Pease, 1985). Furthermore, probation statistics demonstrate that the CSO was beginning to slip down-tariff, with the proportion of first time offenders increasing from 10 per cent in 1981 to 14% in 1991 (Home Office, 1993; see also Hine and Thomas, 1996). Whilst a comprehensive analysis of sentencing practice is beyond the scope of this text, there is a clear inference that the CSO was beginning to attract less serious offenders, who might otherwise have received a fine (Rex and Gelsthorpe, 2002). With the prison population continuing to rise steeply (Home Office, 1988), the government realised that they needed to improve sentencer confidence in CS and community sanctions more generally. This was the beginning of the process that led to the Criminal Justice Act (CJA) 1991 (Home Office, 1990).

The Criminal Justice Act 1991: a tough turning point

By the late 1980s, new retributionist theory had become the most dominant penal theory (Hudson, 2003, p. 39) adopted by policy makers, emphasising that punishment should be commensurate to the seriousness of the offence (see also Von Hirsch, 1993; Von Hirsch and Ashworth, 1998; Garland, 2001; Easton and Piper, 2005; Faulkner and Burnett, 2011). Indeed, the CJA 1991[4] introduced a general sentencing framework which established the principle of proportionality, otherwise known as 'just deserts' (Wasik, 2008, p. 4; Sanders, 1998; see also Woolf and Tumin, 1991; Department of Health and Home Office [Reed Report], 1992; Home Office, 1995a). The Act described three levels of offence seriousness: 'so minor' that a fine or discharge was sufficient; 'serious enough' to warrant a community sentence, or 'so serious' that only a custodial sentence is appropriate (Hudson, 2003; see also Wasik and Taylor, 1991; Worrall and Hoy, 2005; Raynor and Vanstone, 2002).

Perhaps most importantly for CS, the CJA 1991 reconceptualised community sentences and there was a rejection of the 'alternatives to custody model' (Wasik, 2008, p. 4; Muncie, 1999). Instead, community sentences were regarded as distinctive sanctions, warranted through their ability to deliver *punishment* through the attachment of conditions such as tagging and curfew (Muncie, 1999, p. 160; Wasik and von Hirsch, 1988; Worrall and Hoy, 2005). Moreover, the probation service focused on stricter enforcement of all community orders (Muncie, 1999; Gelsthorpe and Rex, 2004; Hudson, 2003; Faulkner and Burnett, 2011).

DOI: 10.1057/9781137400468.0006

This led to an increase in the proportionate use of community sentences at both Crown Court (from 25% in 1992 to 33% in 1993) and magistrates courts (from 20% in 1992 to 28% in 1993) (Home Office, 1995b, p. 144).

Despite this new context, the Home Office continued to stress the re-integrative benefits of CS, arguing that it should be used in a way that *'strengthened not weakened offenders' links with the community'* (Home Office, 1990; 1992, p. 67; 1995a, p. 34). Crucially, however, in reality the CJA 1991 created a clear distinction between probation as *rehabilitation* and CS as *punishment* (Rex and Gelsthorpe. 2002, p. 313; see also Faulkner and Burnett, 2011). This occurred for several reasons. Firstly, there was a legislative rehabilitative requirement (CJA, 1991, section 6) that encouraged probation officers to utilise CS as a restriction of liberty for those unsuitable for probation. Secondly, the Combination Order,[5] introduced within the Act, became popular with magistrates who were able to combine 'help' through probation with 'punishment' through CS (Ellis, Hedderman and Mortimer, 1996, p. 10; Rex and Gelsthorpe, 2002). Arguably, the re-integrative spirit of the CSO, outlined in the 1970s by the Advisory Council, was lost or at least reduced, taking second place to the overriding requirement for community punishment (Rex and Gelsthorpe, 2002; McIvor, 1993; Gelsthorpe and Rex, 2004; Wasik, 2008).

The early 1990s also signified an increasingly punitive juncture in relation to youth justice, to which this chapter now turns. Certainly, the burgeoning popular punitiveness that developed in relation to young offenders at the time, led directly to the introduction of New Labour, the Crime and Disorder Act (CDA) (1998) and most importantly, YJCR (Dugmore, Pickford and Angus, 2006; Stanley, 2001; Pamment, 2010; Rogowski, 2010; Faulkner and Burnett, 2011).

In 1991, there was a period of high profile media coverage surrounding a number of incidents that occurred within English and Welsh cities,[6] using newly coined phrases such as: joyriding; ram-raiding and a major campaign relating to the threat of persistent young offenders (Rogowski, 2010; Campbell, 1993). Most importantly, however, the abduction and murder of two-year-old James Bulger by two ten-year-old boys in February 1993, led to a *'populist crisis'* surrounding not only the crime but young people generally (Dugmore, Pickford and Angus, 2006, p. 44). The crime changed the public's perception of young people and as Muncie, Hughes and McLaughlin (2002) have stated, it seemed that children had *'lost all sense of decency, discipline and morality; their 'innocence'*

DOI: 10.1057/9781137400468.0006

had been 'corrupted' (p. 41). Certainly, the Bulger killing sparked a media-led demonization of youth, a seeming hardening of public attitudes and harsher political responses to young offenders (Jenks, 1996; McNutt, 2010; Stanley, 2001).

Consequently, at a Conservative Party conference in 1993, the then Home Secretary Michael Howard outlined his new criminal justice policy, acknowledging that it would result in an increased use of custody. He famously stated: *'we shall no longer judge the success of our system of justice by a fall in our prison population...let us be clear: prison works'* (cited in Newburn, 2007, p. 666). The Criminal Justice Act 1993 was subsequently introduced, removing much of the earlier CJA 1991 legislation (Home Office, 1995a, p. 216; see also Sanders, 1998). In particular, it reversed the criteria justifying the use of custodial sentences and it allowed full offending history to be disclosed when considering appropriate disposals (Home Office, 1995a, p. 216; Worrall and Hoy, 2005; Hudson, 2003). As Dugmore, Pickford and Angus (2006, p. 44) have stated, the CJA 1993 *'can be viewed as the beginning of a march towards more justice orientated policies within the criminal justice system generally'* (see also Worrall and Hoy, 2005).

It is important to recognise that the 'get tough' approach adopted by the Conservative Party coincided with important underlying political changes at the time (Newburn, 1998). Specifically, the Labour Party in opposition were challenging the [then] Conservative government over its claim to be the party of law and order and what followed was described as an *'unedifying spectacle of the Home Secretary and his Labour Shadow* [Tony Blair] *'fighting to out-tough each other'* (p. 200; see also Bottoms, 1995). The Conservatives who were low in the opinion polls, lurched towards a more punitive response, introducing police detention and secure remand for offenders as young as 12, through the Criminal Justice and Public Order Act 1994 (Home Office, 1995a, p. 217; Dugmore, Pickford and Angus, 2006; Rogowski, 2010; Wasik, 2008).

During the lead up to the general election in 1997, there was certainly an intense period of 'populist punitiveness'. This has been defined as the *'the notion of politicians tapping into, and using for their own purposes, what they believe to be the public's generally punitive stance'* (Bottoms, 1995, p. 40; Raynor and Vanstone, 2002). The notion is closely linked to the classicist view that crime is the result of a choice of action rather than caused by circumstances, and thus deserving of punishment (Dugmore et al., 2006). According to Bottoms (1995) popular punitiveness occurs

DOI: 10.1057/9781137400468.0006

for several reasons. Firstly, it is argued that it can be effective in reducing crime through deterrence and incapacitation. Secondly, it is also said to foster a sense of moral agreement regarding right and wrong. Perhaps most importantly, however, it is an excellent vote winner. As Dugmore *et al.* (2006) have highlighted, in the post Bulger moral panic, it would have been *'electoral suicide for any political party to appear soft on serious and persistent offenders'* (p. 71).

With particular importance to youth justice, in 1995 the Audit Commission started a review of the youth justice system and one year later it delivered its extremely negative findings. In a now famous 'Misspent Youth' report (Audit Commission, 1996), it was argued that the youth justice system was inefficient; unconstructive; spending too much money on expensively processing offenders but not dealing with their offending behaviour; and there was insufficient co-ordination between agencies. It was stated that:

> The current system for dealing with youth crime is inefficient and expensive, while little is being done to deal effectively with juvenile nuisance. The present arrangements are failing young people who are not being guided away from offending to constructive activities...resources need to be shifted from processing young offenders to dealing with their behaviour. At the same time, efforts to prevent offending and other anti social behaviour by young people need to be coordinated between the different agencies involved. (Audit Commission, 1996, p. 96)

The Labour Party certainly capitalised on this finding and argued that under the Conservatives, the youth justice system was in disarray and it proposed a radical change (see also Straw and Michael, 1996; Muncie, 1999; Pamment, 2010). Upon publishing its plans to reform the youth justice system and for preventing youth crime (see Labour Party, 1996: *Tackling Youth Crime: Reforming Youth Justice*, TYCRYJ), the [then] Shadow Home Secretary Jack Straw stated:

> The criminal justice system should work best where it could be most effective-in turning youngsters away from crime, teaching them the difference between right and wrong before it is too late. However, in England and Wales, this system is in advanced decay. It does not work. It can scarcely be called a system at all. It lacks coherent objectives. It satisfies neither those whose prime concern is crime control, nor those whose principle priority is the welfare of the young offender. (Cited in Newburn, 1998, p. 201; see also Labour, 1996, p. 9)

DOI: 10.1057/9781137400468.0006

New Labour, the Crime and Disorder Act 1998 and YJCR

Following New Labour's landslide victory in May 1997, its main legislative priority was the development of its youth justice policy (Jones, 2002) and it embarked on what is considered to be the '*most radical overhaul of the youth justice system in fifty years*' (Goldson, 2000 vii cited by Smith, 2003, p. 227). In particular the Crime and Disorder Act (CDA) 1998 was introduced, described as its 'flagship legislation' (Muncie, 1999, p. 147) and the Youth Justice Criminal Evidence Act (YJCA) 1999 (see Crawford and Newburn, 2002). Both these Acts were outlined in the White Paper, *No more Excuses – A New Approach to Tackling Youth Crime in England and Wales* (Home Office, 1997), bringing in substantial changes to the youth justice system (Crawford and Newburn, 2002; Gray, 2005; Muncie, 1999; Smith, 2003; Pamment, 2010).

Section 37 of the CDA 1998 established the primary aim of the youth justice system: '*to prevent offending by children and young persons*' (Crime and Disorder Act 1998, section 37). This was largely in response to the Audit Commission's earlier criticism that the youth justice system did not have a coherent objective (Audit Commission, 1996). Furthermore, representing a return to 'systemic managerialism' (see Bottoms, 1995), whereby lax management processes are addressed through the efficient standardisation of practice (Dugmore *et al.*, 2006, p. 32; Muncie, 2004), section 39 required local authorities to introduce multi-agency Youth Offending Teams (YOTs).

YOTs have been described as 'teams not belonging to a single department but consisting of representatives from the police, probation, social services, health, education, drugs, alcohol misuse and housing officers' (Souhami, 2007, p. 208; YJB, 2009a; Pamment, 2010; Burnett and Appleton, 2004; Ellis and Boden, 2005). There is now a YOT (sometimes called Youth Offending Service or YOS) in every local authority; 157 at the time of writing, in England and Wales (YJB, 2009a) and they are centrally monitored and controlled by the Youth Justice Board (YJB), an executive non-departmental public body which was also introduced as part of the CDA 1998.

The CDA 1998 introduced a number of measures aimed at 'preemptive early intervention'[7] (see Dugmore *et al.*, 2006), including Anti-Social Behaviour Orders (ASBOs) and Curfew and Child Safety Orders

(CCSOs). Of primary importance to this text, is section 67 which established community reparation (YJCR) through unpaid work for offenders aged 10–17, as an option under the Reparation Order (Holdaway *et al.*, 2001). It is important to note here, that YJCR is also a core element of the Referral Order; introduced within the Youth Justice and Criminal Evidence Act 1999 (Newburn *et al.*, 2002).

As shown in the 1998 sentencing framework (Table 2.1), both the Reparation Order and Referral Order were introduced as 'first-tier' disposals. 'First-tier', 'community' and 'custodial' disposals are given to young offenders by the courts. Conversely, pre-court sanctions, including police reprimands and final warnings, are given for one or more offences detected by the police. According to the YJB (2009b), disposals are split into these four categories based on the seriousness of the disposal (see also Ministry of Justice, 2012a).

The CDA 1998 and introduction of the Reparation Order, was the point at which YJCR and adult CS began to develop in parallel. Certainly, since 2000, both disposals have undergone successive name changes and have been negatively impacted by the political requirement for increased visibility (Carter, 2003; Casey, 2008; YJB, 2010). This chapter now turns to discussing these key changes.

TABLE 2.1   *1998 sentencing framework*

Pre-Court	First Tier	Community Order	Custody
Police Reprimand	Absolute Discharge	Action Plan Order	Detention and Training Order
Final Warning	Conditional Discharge	Attendance Centre Order	Section 90/91
	Bind Over	Community Punishment and Rehabilitation Order	Section 226
	Compensation Order	Community Punishment Order	Section 228
	Fine	Community Rehabilitation Order	
	Referral Order	Community Rehabilitation Order and Conditions	
	Reparation Order	Supervision Order	
	Sentence Deferred	Supervision Order and Conditions	

Source: Developed from Natale, 2010.

DOI: 10.1057/9781137400468.0006

Adult CS and YJCR post 2000: it's time to 'pay back' and 'make good'

In 2000, the Criminal Justice and Court Services Act was introduced and under section 44 (1), the adult CSO was renamed the Community Punishment Order (CPO), once again re-emphasising the punitive, rather than re-integrative aspects of completing unpaid work (Rex and Gelsthorpe, 2002; McIvor, 2002; Gelsthorpe and Rex, 2004; Wasik, 2008). However, in the autumn of 2003, Enhanced Community Punishment (ECP) was launched which aimed to maximise the rehabilitative elements of the sentence, through skills learning; problem solving and pro-social modelling (discussed further in Chapter 3). Whilst probation services made substantial attempts to change their CPO schemes, within months of its introduction, there was a relaxation in ECP requirements, due to escalating costs. After which, probation areas moved away from ECP, towards a more punitive and, what was seen as, a more cost effective approach (Ministry of Justice, 2010a, pp. 5–6).

In order to provide a more flexible sentencing structure, the Criminal Justice Act (CJA) 2003 introduced a generic Community Order (CO) (see Mair and Mills, 2009). This is currently utilised for offenders aged 18 and over and it can last between 12 days and three years (Wasik, 2008; Solomon and Silvestri, 2008; Kaye and Gibbs, 2010). Crucially, the CJA 2003 abolished the CPO / ECP and adult CS was renamed *'unpaid work'*, becoming one of 12 potential requirements[8] of the CO. It is important to recognise that unpaid work can be utilised as a single requirement (stand alone) or as one of two or more requirements (multiple requirement order: see Solomon and Silvestri, 2008, p. 9). However, the stand-alone unpaid work requirement is most popular, representing 29% of all community orders (see Ministry of Justice, 2015a).

Unpaid work is currently promoted to the public under the brand of *'Community Payback'* (Ministry of Justice, 2010; Solomon and Silvestri, 2008). This important development originated from a Cabinet Review conducted in 2008, whereby a survey discovered that the public do not see *'enough visible action being taken to challenge, catch and punish criminals...Too much work is invisible'*[9] (Casey, 2008, p. 53; see also Carter, 2003). Within the review, 71% of respondents agreed that offenders' work should be more visible. Crucially however, only 52% specified that this could be achieved through high visibility clothing (Casey, 2008, p. 53).[10]

DOI: 10.1057/9781137400468.0006

Nevertheless, as a result of the Casey Review (2008) offenders on unpaid work are now required to wear highly visible orange vests with '*Community Payback*' emblazoned on the back to identify and shame them (Maruna and King, 2008; see also Pamment and Ellis, 2010; National Association of Probation Officers, NAPO, 2008; 2009; 2010; Brooker, 2008). Additionally, Casey argued that the activities undertaken must be more demanding, '*not something the public would choose to do themselves*' (Casey, 2008, p. 55; Maruna and King, 2008).

The National Association of Probation Officers (NAPO) promptly called for the withdrawal of the *Community Payback* vests,[11] arguing that they are demeaning, excluding and potentially dangerous (NAPO, 2008; 2009; 2010). In fact, NAPO quickly catalogued a number of incidents that have occurred during the work placements and in some areas the use of vests has been suspended (see Milanian, 2009). For example, offenders have been verbally abused, objects have been thrown at workers and community service vans have been followed. NAPO (2008) has argued that the primary intention of the vests is to make the government look tougher on crime and demean offenders. However, they warn that the initiative could lead to an increase in breach rates and the use of custody.

Academics have also been highly critical of the Casey review and the *Community Payback* scheme. Maruna and King (2008, p. 345) identify that the concept of reparation is popular with members of the public. However, they argue that Casey (2008) misunderstands this and throughout the review is extremely punitive, creating a substantial distinction between law abiding citizens and criminals (Maruna and King, 2008, p. 346). Furthermore, there is a strong implication that community service should be '*degrading, demeaning and shaming*'. Indeed, as Maruna and King (2008, p. 34) state: '*The term payback is used as a sort of double entendre to refer not just to restitution, but also to retribution as in the phrase it's payback time!*'

The most experienced researcher on CS for adult offenders in England and Wales, Gill McIvor (2010, p. 55), has also criticised the introduction of *Community Payback* stating that it '*evokes strong connotations of vengefulness that would appear to forefront retributive aims*' (see also NACRO, 2005). She supports the notion that the 'repackaging' was a political attempt to gain wider public and judicial support for custodial reductionism and notes the important negative role played by the media. In particular, McIvor (2010, p. 55) cites several previous attempts by journalists to highlight the leniency of CS, including an article published in the Sunday Mail entitled: '*Cons on Community Service filmed boozing, smoking and using phones*' (see also Fricker, 2008). It is therefore argued that the introduction of *Community Payback* is designed to raise public confidence or media representation of it and allay any fears that the government is 'soft on crime' (McIvor, 2010; Bottoms, 2008). However, others have argued that the idea has the danger of eroding the underlying re-integrative spirit of community service (Maruna and King, 2008; McIvor, 1993; Pamment and Ellis, 2010).

As previously noted, YJCR has developed in a similar manner to adult CS. In fact, the Criminal Justice and Immigration Act 2008 introduced the Youth Rehabilitation Order (YRO). This is the generic community sentence,[12] providing a menu of 19 'flexible' interventions for tackling offending behaviour (YJB, 2009b). One of which is community reparation which comes under the 'activity' requirement. However, as shown in the current sentencing framework (Table 2.2), YJCR remains a core component of the 'first tier' Reparation Order and Referral Order (YJB, 2011 see also Newburn *et al.*, 2002; Holdaway *et al.*, 2001).

In 2013/14, the majority of young people were given community reparation through Referral Orders, with 12,606 issued. Indeed, young offenders given Reparation Orders represent a minority, with only 271 issued over the same period (Ministry of Justice, 2015b). The primary research within this book reveals a similar picture, as 67% of the young offender sample was subject to Referral Orders, followed by Reparation Orders (20.2%) and ISSPs (7.4%) (see Chapter 4).

Similarly to adult CS and the *Community Payback* initiative, YJCR has undergone a rebranding and in 2010 it was promoted to the public under the banner of '*Making Good*' (YJB, 2010). This development can also be traced back to Louise Casey's recommendation for increased visibility, as outlined above (see Casey, 2008). The *Making Good* strategy involves community participation, whereby members of the public suggest reparative activities that could be undertaken by young offenders (YJB, 2010; Pamment and Ellis, 2010). These suggestions are then considered and implemented, where appropriate, by local YOTs.

The YJB has argued that '*Making Good*' provides a valuable opportunity to engage with the wider community (YJB, 2010). However, the strategy has attracted critical attention, for instance the [then] Shadow Home Justice Secretary Dominic Grieve reportedly rejected it as a 'gimmick' (Pemberton, 2010). Furthermore, the policy director at the Centre for

TABLE 2.2 *Current sentencing framework*

Pre-Court	Final Warning	First Tier	Youth Rehabilitation Order		Custody
Police Reprimand		Absolute Discharge	Activity Requirement	Education Requirement	Detention and Training Order
Final Warning		Conditional Discharge	Supervision Requirement	Prohibited Activity Requirement	Section 90/91
		Bind Over	Curfew Requirement	Electronic Monitoring Requirement	Section 226
		Compensation Order	Programme Requirement	Drug Testing Requirement	Section 228
		Fine	Residence Requirement (16 / 17 year olds only)	Drug Treatment Requirement	
		Referral Order	Mental Health Treatment Requirement	LA Residence Requirement	
		Reparation Order	Attendance Centre Requirement	Unpaid Work Requirement (16 / 17 year olds only)	
		Sentence Deferred	Exclusion Requirement	Intoxicating Substance Treatment Requirement	

Source: Developed from Natale, 2010.

DOI: 10.1057/9781137400468.0006

Crime and Justice Studies, Will McMahon, labelled the policy as a '*criminal justice version of the X-factor*'. He further stated, '*We are dealing with a group of troubling, and troubled, young people and it's not clear that subjecting their punishment activities to a public poll via a website will benefit them*' (see Pemberton, 2010).

The notion of '*making good*' is synonymous with restorative justice (RJ) (Marshall, 1999; Mantle *et al.*, 2005; Dugmore *et al.*, 2006; Zedner, 1994; Sumner, 2006). In fact, the YJB has stressed that YJCR is a key component of its RJ strategy (see YJB, 2006; 2010; Dugmore *et al.*, 2006; Kerslake, 2011; Holdaway *et al.*, 2001; Gray, 2005). Whilst a comprehensive coverage of RJ within a youth justice context is beyond the remit of this book (see instead Stephenson, Giller and Brown, 2007; Crawford and Newburn, 2002; Gavrielides, 2008), it is important to briefly outline how community reparation relates to the broader RJ framework.

Defining RJ is, unsurprisingly, contentious (Gray, 2005; Gavrielides, 2008; Wilcox and Hoyle, 2004; Miers *et al.*, 2001). However, an internationally recognised definition states that it '*is a process whereby parties with a stake in a specific offence collectively resolve how to deal with the aftermath of the offence and its implications for the future*' (Marshall, 1999, p. 6). A broader definition provided by Stephenson, Giller and Brown (2007, p. 161), argues that RJ brings victims and offenders together through direct or indirect contact. As a consequence, it is hoped that such an approach will encourage a greater understanding by the offender of the negative impact of criminal behaviour, thus prompting desistance from offending in the future (see also Hayden and Gough, 2010).

There are a substantial number of programmes within the youth justice system in England and Wales identified as 'restorative' (Wilcox and Hoyle, 2004). However, it is possible to judge the level of restoration offered by examining the extent to which they encourage discourse between victims; offenders and their communities. McCold and Watchel (2003, p. 3) state that: '*only when all three primary stakeholders are actively involved...is a process fully restorative*'. Thus community reparation has been classed as 'partly restorative', due to the lack of victim involvement and the focus on offender responsibilisation[13] (see also Walgrave, 1999; Roche, 2001; Barry, McNeil and Lightowler, 2009).

Wilcox and Hoyle (2004, p. 16) are keen to highlight that those interventions deemed 'partly restorative' are not any less effective, but they differ from the usual principles associated with RJ. More contentiously

DOI: 10.1057/9781137400468.0006

for this book, Holdaway *et al.* (2001, p. 101) argue that community reparation is the least valuable disposal for offenders, the work more associated with retribution. Furthermore, Stephenson, Giller and Brown (2007, p. 164) stress that only face-to-face contact with victims (i.e. fully restorative) lead to reductions in re-offending. Certainly, there is a clear inference here, that community reparation is ineffective, due to its limited status as a restorative sanction.

It is important to acknowledge, however, that RJ works differently with different types of offenders. In particular, there is evidence to suggest that the process works more effectively with serious and violent criminals, rather than with low-level offenders (see Sherman and Strang, 2007). Therefore, a presumption that restorative interventions are effective for the majority of offenders is fundamentally incorrect (see also Robinson and Shapland, 2008; Dignan, 2005; Ellis and Savage, 2012). Moreover, community reparation is rejected (Holdaway *et al.*, 2001; Stephenson *et al.*, 2007) before adequate consideration of other protective factors that prevent recidivism, which the disposal may develop (see also Zedner, 1994; Sumner, 2006). The following section aims to address this, by briefly exploring how the completion of unpaid work may support adult and young offenders in the acquisition of employability skills (Gelsthorpe and Rex, 2004; Home Office, 2004).

Unpaid work and the acquisition of employability skills

The development of this book did take account of findings from the vast body of desistance literature. Indeed, a key conclusion from Maruna's (2001) work, is that desistance from crime correlates directly with obtaining work (see also Sampson and Laub, 1993; Farrall, 2002). However, the focus of desistance theory is largely on longitudinal factors, such as: the importance of ageing, offenders gaining and maintaining stable employment, forming social bonds and improving narrative identity (Maruna, 2001; Sampson and Laub, 2003; Matza, 1969). Some of this change also occurs beyond the end of criminal justice sanctions. Furthermore, whilst desistance theory provides a descriptive analysis of the influences underpinning offender change, it currently lacks an organised framework and it is not readily translated into prescriptions for practice. This study is focused more narrowly on the practice-based relationship between supervision content and offenders' attitudes during the disposal period.

DOI: 10.1057/9781137400468.0006

Therefore, it concentrates on the evidence drawn from the 'what works' literature, outlined below.

The extensive reform programme of the late 1990s outlined previously, involved the introduction of *'what works'* or *'evidence-based'* principles, to ensure that interventions with both adult and young offenders were effective (Lipsey, 1992; Palmer, 1992; Burnett and Roberts, 2004; Francis and Padel, 2000; Barry, 2000; McCulloch, 2010). There is now a large body of literature that identifies ways of working with offenders that reduce re-offending rates, which has become the 'gold standard' of effectiveness in England and Wales. These have included many studies of individual programmes; meta-analytical assessments of a number of similar evaluations (see Glass *et al.*, 1981; Hunter and Schmidt, 1990; Lipsey, 1995), and systematic literature reviews (Mulvey, Arthur and Reppucci, 1993; Sherman *et al.*, 1997; Andrews, 1995; McGuire, 1995; Chapman and Hough, 1998; Utting and Vennard, 2000).

One of the main findings to emerge from the *'what works'* initiative was that Cognitive Behavioural Therapy (CBT) generally produced the greatest reductions in recidivism (Garrett, 1985; Ross and Fabiano, 1985; Lipsey, Chapman and Landenberger, 2001; Farrall, 2004; Merrington and Stanley, 2000; Ellis and Winstone, 2002; Burnett and Roberts, 2004; Goggin and Gendreau, 2006). CBT involves 'treating' distorted or deficit thought processes, through techniques encouraging self-control; anger management; critical reasoning; emotional management and improved social skills (Clark, 2000; McGuire, 1995; Gorman, 2001; Hedderman and Sugg, 1997; Ellis and Winstone, 2002; Kendall, 2004; Lipsey *et al.*, 2007).

Certainly, the spotlight has been on 'treatment' CBT over the past 25 years (Ross and Fabiano, 1985; Grubin and Thornton, 1994; Gorman, 2001; Ellis and Winstone, 2002; Kendall, 2004; see also Faulkner and Burnett, 2011). However, the *'what works'* evidence largely centred on the importance of developing offenders' employability skills, as part of 'multi-modal' programmes (Rutter, Giller and Hagell, 1998; McGuire, 1995; Farrall, 2002; Hollin and Palmer, 2006). In fact, the results of a large-scale meta-analysis of 400 research studies indicate that the most effective interventions for reducing recidivism focus on training and skills, suitable for employment (Lipsey, 1995, pp. 76–77; see also Farrington, 1996; 1997; Farrall, 2002; Hollin and Palmer, 2006).

It is widely accepted that a major contributing factor to the onset of criminality is a lack of general skills relevant to work (May, 1999; Downes, 1993; Sampson and Laub, 1993; Home Office, 2004; Nescot

DOI: 10.1057/9781137400468.0006

Report, 2007; Mair and May, 1997; Stephenson; Giller and Brown, 2007). Indeed, research has shown that 70% of offenders entering custody are not in training or employment and have very limited basic skills (Niven and Stewart, 2005; see also May, 1999; Social Exclusion Unit, 2002; Knott, 2004; Home Office, 2004; Nescot Report, 2007). Thus, interventions offering skills acquisition, qualifications and experience provide a valuable contribution to offenders desisting from crime (Carter and Pycroft, 2010, p. 213; Sarno *et al.*, 1999; Home Office, 2004; Carter, 2007; Lewis *et al.*, 2007; Shaw and Cantrell, 2008; Bain and Parkinson, 2010).

Although unpaid work is rejected for its limited RJ status (Holdaway *et al.*, 2001, p. 101; Stephenson *et al.*, 2007), academics have recognised that the intervention represents a 'natural environment' for the acquisition of employability skills, a far greater factor correlated with the '*what works*' literature (Rex, 2001, p. 80; Carter and Pycroft, 2010, pp. 14–16). For the purposes of this text, employability skills refer to the following broad categories: *transferable*; *problem solving*; *team working* and *communication* skills (adapted from Carter and Pycroft, 2010, pp. 14–16; see also Work Foundation, 2010; Chartered Institute of Personnel and Development, CIPD, 2004).

Firstly and perhaps most importantly, unpaid work *could* enhance transferable skills, whereby offenders are gaining knowledge of key vocational trades such as concreting, fencing, painting or decorating. Upon completion of the activities, offenders *could* gain certificates and qualifications in preparation for employment (Carter and Pycroft, 2010, p. 228). The work may also encourage offenders to adopt a problem solving approach, by identifying advantages or disadvantages of varying techniques and by following health and safety guidelines (McIvor, 2002, p. 4; Carter and Pycroft, 2010, p. 228). Ultimately, this could lead to increased confidence; self efficacy and motivation to change (Gelsthorpe and Rex, 2004, p. 235; see also Advisory Council on the Penal System, 1970, p. 13).

Unpaid work *may* also encourage team working skills, where the activities develop trusting relationships between co-workers and supervisors, whilst working within potentially hazardous environments (Carter and Pycroft, 2010, p. 228). This may enhance communication and develop socially responsible behaviour (Rethinking Crime and Punishment, 2005, p. 2; see also Advisory Council on the Penal System, 1970, p. 13; Tallant, Sambrook and Green, 2008, p. 79).

One model of intervention that can be exploited in this way is Pro-Social Modelling (PSM) (see Trotter, 1993; 1999; HMIP, 1998;

Raynor, 1998). PSM emerged from probation practice, through practitioner-research and it has been most extensively developed in Australia. It has been defined as, '*the practice of offering praise and rewards for...pro-social expressions and actions*' (Trotter, 1993, p. 4). According to Trotter (1999, pp. 67–73), there are four stages in the PSM approach: Pro-social comments and actions are identified; rewards are provided; pro-social behaviours are modelled and undesirable behaviours are challenged (see also Tallant, Sambrook and Green, 2008; Chapman and Hough, 1998).

Pro-social modelling could occur during unpaid work in several ways. In particular, supervisory staff might act as positive role models, guiding and improving performance, as well as rewarding success and neutralising pro-criminal attitudes (McIvor, 2002; McCulloch, 2010). In addition, during work team placements meaningful dialogue could occur between fellow workers; supervising staff and beneficiaries. Upon completion of their tasks, offenders could see the impact of their work, gaining a sense of achievement. This might lead to increased self-esteem; empathy and most importantly, a positive change in identity (Rex and Gelsthorpe, 2002; McIvor, 2002; McIvor and Barry, 1998; 2000; Maruna, 2001; Mercier and Alarie, 2002; Stenner and Taylor, 2008; Carter and Pycroft, 2010).

Proponents of PSM argue that it is a highly constructive and powerful approach and it has been described as a core ingredient, which engages offenders and encourages positive behavioural change (Andrews *et al.*, 1979; Chapman and Hough, 1998; Home Office, 2006; Trotter, 1999; McIvor, 2002; McCulloch, 2010). However, to others, PSM is simplistic and superficial (Tallant, Sambrook and Green, 2008), and the process is entirely dependent upon the attitude of supervisors (Carter and Pycroft, 2010). Nonetheless, little is known about its use, implementation and potential within the context of unpaid work (McCulloch, 2010).

In summary, the focus of unpaid work is neither specifically on offending behaviour nor on restorative justice (Holdaway *et al.*, 2001; Stephenson *et al.*, 2007; McCulloch, 2010). Crucially however, the practical setting and nature of the communication that takes place: '*might well offer learning experiences at least as powerful as an approach that directly tackles offending behaviour*' (Rex, 2001, p. 80; McIvor, 2002; Chapman and Hough, 1998; McCulloch, 2010). Thus, Chapter 3 systematically examines whether adult CS and YJCR is effective in reducing recidivism. The final section below provides a brief review of the key themes identified within this chapter.

DOI: 10.1057/9781137400468.0006

Review

When adult CS was introduced in 1972, it was hoped that the disposal would be re-integrative *and* [emphasis added] rehabilitative (Advisory Council on the Penal System, 1970; Hine and Thomas, 1996; Rex and Gelsthorpe, 2002). In fact, the Advisory committee (1970, par 34) was confident that it would contribute to a changed outlook on the part of the offender. Furthermore, it was stated that CS should not be seen as *'wholly negative or punitive'* (see also McIvor, 1993). However, as McCulloch (2010, p. 4) has previously stated, *'the initial vision of CS is barely recognisable in the practice that has followed – a practice which, at least officially, has tended to capitalise on the punitive aspects and appeal of CS'*. Indeed, successive legislative changes have now placed a more substantial emphasis on the retributive power of adult CS, perhaps at the expense of both reintegration and rehabilitation.

Under the CJA 1991, there was a rejection of the 'alternatives to custody model' (Wasik, 2008; Muncie, 1999). Adult CS was reconceptualised as a distinctive sanction and rebranded, placing particular emphasis on its 'tough' punitive function (see CJA, 1991 section 6; McIvor, 2002; Worrall and Hoy, 2005). The Act also introduced the Combination Order, reinforcing and combining a distinction between probation as *rehabilitation* and CS as *punishment*. Thus, the disposal quickly became synonymous only with its retributive element (McIvor, 1993; Ellis, Hedderman and Mortimer, 1996; Rex and Gelsthorpe, 2002; Gelsthorpe and Rex, 2004; Wasik, 2008; Faulkner and Burnett, 2011).

A decade later, the CSO was renamed the Community Punishment Order, further emphasising the retributive aspect only (Rex and Gelsthorpe, 2002; McIvor, 2002). Through the Criminal Justice Act 2003, unpaid work is now a condition of a generic Community Order, promoted to the public under the label of *'Community Payback'*. This politically inspired initiative (Casey, 2008) has firmly positioned adult CS as a 'marginalised' retributive disposal in England and Wales, where little attention is now paid to the possibility that it may have greater re-integrative and rehabilitative potential on offenders (McIvor, 2002; Rex and Gelsthorpe, 2002; Maruna and King, 2008; Pamment and Ellis, 2010; National Association of Probation Officers, NAPO, 2008).

YJCR has a much shorter history, introduced by New Labour under the CDA 1998 (Crime and Disorder Act, 1998, p.s. 67). This followed the Criminal Justice and Public Order Bill (1994). It is important to note

DOI: 10.1057/9781137400468.0006

here, therefore, that YJCR was introduced at a time when retribution was already the main focus established for adult CS (Rex and Gelsthorpe, 2002; Maruna and King, 2008; Wasik, 2008). Thus, since its inception, it has developed in a similar manner to adult CS. In particular, the Youth Rehabilitation Order (YRO) has placed YJCR as an option, providing a further distinction between *rehabilitation* and *punishment*. Additionally, the *'Making Good'* scheme mirrored the *'Community Payback'* strategy within adult CS, whereby the political requirement for increased visibility and public participation has become a key focus (Casey, 2008; YJB, 2010; see also Pamment and Ellis, 2010).

Perhaps most importantly, YJCR appears to be prematurely dismissed before its potential benefits have been considered. Whilst the reparative aspect of YJCR has given the disposal a restorative element, it has been criticised for the weak level of restoration that it provides, the work becoming more incorporated with retribution (Holdaway *et al.*, 2001; Wilcox and Hoyle, 2004; Haines and O'Mahony, 2006; Stephenson, Giller and Brown, 2007). However, this is only one facet and it misses the possibility that the disposal may develop employability skills, a far greater factor correlated with the 'what works' evidence base (Rutter, Giller and Hagell, 1998; McGuire, 1995; Farrall, 2002; Hollin and Palmer, 2006).

In 2002, Rex and Gelsthorpe argued the need to rediscover the rehabilitative and re-integrative potential of unpaid work, the pursuit of which would take the sanction back to its origin (p. 311; Advisory Council on the Penal System, 1970, p. par 34; McCulloch, 2010). They further highlighted the potential for developing elements of the sanction that could influence long-term behavioural change, specifically the acquisition of employability skills. They went on to argue that the retributive focus should not exclude the re-integrative aims, advocating harmonisation between work and the development of skills suitable for employment (Rex and Gelsthorpe, 2002, p. 311; see also McIvor, 1991; 1992).

Although the current political focus is on retribution, there may be unintended benefits for the sanction. Consecutive governments have stressed a commitment to adult CS and YJCR, advocating greater and immediate use, increased hours, tougher conditions and diversification of new rehabilitation providers, through the voluntary and private sectors (Ministry of Justice, 2012b; Solomon and Silvestri, 2008; YJB,

DOI: 10.1057/9781137400468.0006

2009c; YJB, 2008). This may result in the allocation of further resources, enabling the development and promotion of the more potent elements of the disposal that could promote desistance (i.e. work-based skills). However, to end on a cautionary note, this would necessitate the provision of a *range* of meaningful and engaging tasks, which encourage and facilitate the acquisition of employability skills. The next chapter takes a systematic look at the evidence of whether adult CS and YJCR are effective in reducing re-offending.

Notes

1   CS was introduced in Scotland in 1979 (see Hine and Thomas, 1996; McIvor, 2010).
2   Today, the 'unpaid work requirement' within the generic Community Order is only available for adult offenders aged 18 and above. However, the Youth Rehabilitation Order, supervised by YOTs, has introduced an 'unpaid work requirement' for offenders aged 16–17 years.
3   For comprehensive statistics relating to CS in Europe (see Aebi; DelGrande and Marguet, 2009).
4   Implemented on 1 October 1992 (Home Office, 1995a).
5   The Combination Order combined probation and community service (see Mair, Cross and Taylor, 2007).
6   In particular, Oxford, Cardiff and Tyneside (see Rogowski, 2010).
7   Although many academics are critical of the way it stigmatises and excludes young people (for further discussion see Muncie, 1999; Vaughan, 2000).
8   Unpaid work; Supervision; Accredited programme; Drug rehabilitation; Alcohol treatment; Mental health treatment; Residence; Specified activity; Prohibited activity; Exclusion; Curfew; Attendance centre (see Mair and Mills, 2009).
9   See also: Visible Unpaid Work Strategy (VUWS) (National Probation Service, 2005; Johnson and Ingram, 2007; Bottoms, 2008).
10   Research has shown that the public are not as punitive as sentencers and politicians assume. For instance, a study conducted in 2003 demonstrates that the public feel that the penal system should give paramount importance to rehabilitation (see Hough and Roberts, 2004).
11   Dubbed the 'vests of shame' by the popular press: see Roper (2008).
12   Replacing the following orders: Action Plan Order; Curfew Order; Supervision Order; Community Punishment Order; Community Punishment and Rehabilitation Order; Attendance Centre Order; Drug

DOI: 10.1057/9781137400468.0006

Treatment and Testing Order; Community Rehabilitation Order; Exclusion Order

13   Described as the 'new rehabilitation' of the risk era (for a comprehensive discussion see: Kemshall, 2002; Robinson, 2002; O'Malley, 2001 and Gray, 2005). It is closely linked to the notion of communitarianism, emphasising that the solution to crime is the responsibility of communities and individuals (Dugmore *et al.*, 2006; Barry, McNeil and Lightowler, 2009).

DOI: 10.1057/9781137400468.0006

3

Realising the Potential: The Research Evidence Base for Unpaid Work

Abstract: *This chapter reviews and integrates the research evidence base for unpaid work. It begins by examining national reconviction data relating to the adult Community Service Order (CSO), before exploring the quality and findings of the few studies which have investigated the re-integrative potential of this sanction. The chapter then turns to the youth justice Reparation Order (RO), examining recidivism rates from official statistics and previous research studies. It concludes by identifying both the extent to which policy and practice match the evidence base, and the extent to which they are lacking. It also concludes that there is a paucity of high quality research into community reparation for young offenders.*

Pamment, Nicholas. *Community Reparation for Young Offenders: Perceptions, Policy and Practice.* Basingstoke: Palgrave Macmillan, 2016. DOI: 10.1057/9781137400468.0007.

Reconviction results: a cautionary note

Before looking at the reconviction results of the adult CSO, it is important to bear in mind the caveats that surround this well established field. It is widely accepted that reconviction rates are a substitute for an unidentified level of re-offending. External factors such as victim willingness to report; police efficiency and the decisions of the Crown Prosecution Service (CPS) all impact upon the accuracy of reconviction rates (Spicer and Glicksman, 2004). Nevertheless, such data remains highly useful when examining the effectiveness of court sentences (Kershaw, 1999; Wilcox and Hoyle, 2004). Indeed, as Lloyd *et al.* (1994) have argued, reconviction rates provide the only way of assessing the national impact of custodial and community penalties (p. viii).

It is also important to note the difficulty in analysing the effect of particular disposals, due to their changing use over time (see Ministry of Justice, 2011b). For instance, as shown in the previous chapter, adult community service is now the 'unpaid' work requirement of a broader community order and not a discrete disposal in its own right, as it was originally conceived (Mair and Mills, 2009; Ministry of Justice, 2011b). Similarly, within youth justice, community reparation is a component of the Referral Order and of the Youth Rehabilitation Order (YRO) (YJB, 2010). This makes it difficult to disentangle the effects of unpaid work from the broader 'parent' disposal. In order to ensure a clear focus, this text therefore concentrates on evidence based on the 'stand alone' CSO and Community Punishment Order (CPO) for adult offenders and the analogous Reparation Order within youth justice.

Adult community service order: reconviction results

In the adult system, before the Criminal Justice Act 2003 created a generic community penalty with varying components, the focus was on comparisons between the three main criminal justice disposals: custody; probation and CSOs. As Table 3.1 shows, community service consistently achieved lower reconviction rates over two years compared to custody and probation orders with requirements, and the same is almost true when compared to probation with no requirements. The overall importance of the data presented in Table 3.1 is that it shows a remarkably positive pattern for CSO reconviction rates since the mid-90s, despite significant

DOI: 10.1057/9781137400468.0007

TABLE 3.1   *Comparison of 'raw' adult reconviction figures 1983–2003* (Custody, Probation, Probation with 4A/4B requirements *and* Community Service) *[%]*

Study	Total sample	Time span	Custody	Probation	Probation with 4A/4B requirements	CSO
Home Office (1983, p. 9)	2,486 (tracked 1979)	2 years	64	54	–	53
Home Office (1993, p. 10)	11,062 (tracked 1987)	2 years	–	50	65	54
Raynor and Vanstone (1996, p. 280)	1,991+ (655)	2 years	56	61	–	49
Scottish Executive (2001, p. 20)	54,712 (tracked 1995)	2 years	61	56	–	40
Scottish Executive (2003, p. 12)	53,819 (tracked 1997)	2 years	62	59	–	45
Shepherd and Whiting (2006, p. 19)	53,282 (tracked 2003)	2 years	66	60.6	–	40[1]
Cunliffe and Shepherd (2007, p. 21)	47,084 (tracked 2004)	2 years	64.7	56.9	–	37.9[2]

Notes: [1] Relates to Community Punishment Order.
[2] Relates to Community Punishment Order.

variations in methodologies, sample sizes and jurisdictions, thus highlighting the possibility that adult community service has a beneficial impact upon recidivism (McIvor, 2002; Rex and Gelsthorpe, 2002).

The reconviction data presented above provides a useful indication of the relative performance of community service against other disposals. However, firm conclusions drawn from an inevitable comparison are unreliable (Lloyd *et al.*, 1994; Spicer and Glicksman, 2004; Ministry of Justice, 2011b). Whilst a comprehensive discussion surrounding the methodologies employed within reconviction studies is beyond the scope of this book,[1] it is important to recognise that a simple comparison of 'raw' reconviction figures relating to different types of sentence is erroneous. Indeed, offender characteristics have not been controlled for, especially the level of seriousness of the offence for which they have been convicted (Kershaw, 1999; Lloyd *et al.*, 1994; McIvor, 2010).

More reliable reconviction studies therefore make adjustment for differences in offender characteristics (Carter, Klein and Day, 1992; Kershaw,

DOI: 10.1057/9781137400468.0007

1999; McIvor, 2010; Ministry of Justice, 2012d). This is achieved through the use of logistic regression, whereby variables are utilised to produce an equation which predicts the probability of an outcome, making relative comparisons between different disposals more reliable (for further detail, see Lloyd *et al.*, 1994; Hosmer and Lemeshaw, 2000; Menard, 2002). Expected reconviction rates for a particular group of offenders can thus be calculated, based upon factors other than sentence. These could include age; sex and criminal history (Spicer and Glicksman, 2004). The 'actual' rate of reconviction is then compared to the 'predicted' rate and if significantly lower than expected, it suggests that the sanction is more effective than others in lowering reconviction (Lloyd *et al.*, 1994).

In 1994, Lloyd *et al.* undertook such a study, whereby two-year reconviction rates were examined relating to probation orders; probation orders with 4A/4B requirements (i.e. the more serious attendance at a probation centre); imprisonment and CSOs. Data regarding 18,000 offenders was obtained from the Home Office Probation Index, Prison Index and Offenders Index and expected reconviction rates were calculated with regards to: age; sex; offence type; number of previous appearances in court; rate of appearance; average number of prior convictions and number of youth custody sentences (see Lloyd *et al.*, 1994, p. x).

Unsurprisingly, Lloyd *et al.* (1994, p. 39) found that disposal groups varied greatly in offender characteristics. As shown in Table 3.2, with reference to age, offenders given CSOs and 4A/4B orders were particularly high risk groups, with around half of these people being aged between 17 and 20, compared with 35% of prisoners and 43% of probationers. In all other categories, offenders on 4A/4B orders were shown to be the highest risk group with a larger proportion having six or more previous court appearances, experience of youth imprisonment, a previous appearance rate of ten or more and having been convicted of burglary, theft, criminal damage or motoring offences. Overall, it would appear that offenders on CSOs had very similar characteristics to that of the straight probation group (Lloyd *et al.*, 1994, p. 39).

CSOs achieved a reconviction rate of 49% (see Table 3.3), which was lower than predicted (52%) but not significantly so, when considering age; sex and criminal history of offenders. Conversely, incarceration (54%) and probation with 4A and 4B requirements (63%) did worse than expected (53% and 60% respectively). Therefore, there is an indication that CSOs and probation have a small positive effect, whilst prison and 4A/4B orders have a small negative effect on reconviction (Lloyd *et al.*, 1994, p. 43; see also Raynor and Vanstone, 1996, p. 279).

DOI: 10.1057/9781137400468.0007

TABLE 3.2   *Offender characteristics within the four disposal groups [%]*

Variable	Prisons	CSOs	4A/4Bs	Probation
Age 17–20	35	50	49	43
6+ previous appearances	45	26	47	28
Previous youth imprisonment	44	30	48	27
Previous appearance rate 10+	38	29	45	30
High risk offences (burglary; theft criminal damage; motor offences)	61	77	84	77
Total N	8,179	2,252	3,094	1,803

Source: Adapted from Lloyd *et al.*, 1994, p. 39.

TABLE 3.3   *Two-year reconviction rates for community penalties and custody [%]*

Sentence group	Actual reconvicted	Predicted reconvicted	Total number
Prison	54	53	9,615
Community penalties	47	49	8,196
Probation	43	45	2,448
CSOs	49	52	2,394
4A/4B	63	60	3,354

Source: Adapted from Lloyd *et al.*, 1994, p. 43.

Crucially, with such small differences in the actual and predicted figures (3 percentage points in the case of community service), firm conclusions cannot be made. Moreover, there is a further weakness in the study relating to a lack of dynamic social factor data, such as drug use or marital and employment status (Lloyd *et al.*, 1994; May, 1999). However, the effect of this addition appears to be slight (see May, 1999; Hine and Celnick, 2001).

Five years later, May (1999) undertook a new two-year reconviction study into community sanctions (probation; probation with requirements; CSOs and combination orders) and data was examined from 1993 on more than 7,000 offenders, within six probation service areas. Most importantly, this was the first large scale British study to explore the influence of social circumstances on the prediction of reconviction (May, 1999). In addition to the criminal history of offenders, 'dynamic' social factors were examined such as drug misuse; accommodation; employment; physical and mental health; marital status and responsibilities. 'Static' factors (characteristics which cannot be altered); including ethnicity and previous experience of abuse were also examined (see May, 1999, pp. 5–8 for further detail on methodology).

DOI: 10.1057/9781137400468.0007

Similar to the findings of Lloyd *et al.* (1994) above, May (1999, p. 40) found that offenders given probation with 4A/4B requirements had larger proportions of high risk characteristics than the other disposal groups (see Table 3.4). This was followed by straight probation, combination orders and lastly, CSOs. As May (1999, p. 40) identified, probation was being utilised for more serious offenders and community service for the less serious. Thus, it is important to note here, that consecutive legislative changes (CJA, 1991; 1993) appear to have reversed the original aim of the CSO as an alternative to custody (Hine and Thomas, 1996; see also Advisory Council on the Penal System, 1970).

Following logistic regression analysis to equal out seriousness (Lloyd *et al.*, 1994; Hosmer and Lemeshaw, 2000; Menard, 2002), the community service sample achieved an actual reconviction rate of 42.7%, significantly lower than predicted when considering criminal history variables (44.6%) and the additional influence of social factors (43.7 %) (Table 3.5). Crucially however, straight probation and combination orders performed significantly worse than predicted (May, 1999, p. 46).

A further study on actual and predicted reconviction rates including community service was undertaken six years later (Spicer and Glicksman, 2004). Whilst differences in offender seriousness were controlled for using logistic regression, the study was only able to consider a limited range of static factors for which data was available, including age; gender; offence type and criminal history. The authors do not provide a breakdown of offender characteristics against disposal, but they do state

TABLE 3.4   *A comparison of offender characteristics by disposal (males only) [%]*

Variable	Straight probation	Probation with requirements	CSO	Combination Order
Aged 17–20	26	25	26	28
6+ previous guilty appearances	44	49	31	40
Previous youth imprisonment	36	37	25	37
Previous appearance rate of 10+	43	48	31	39
High risk offences (burglary, theft, criminal damage, motor offences)	45	41	40	39
Unemployed	57	56	41	56
Alcohol/drugs problems	47	52	21	40
Accommodation problems	27	26	12	24
Financial problems	44	25	30	38
N	2,240	422	3,400	641

Source: Adapted from May, 1999, p. 40.

DOI: 10.1057/9781137400468.0007

TABLE 3.5   *Actual and predicted reconviction rates by disposal (criminal history and social variables)*

Sentence	Actual percentage reconvicted	Predicted percentage reconvicted (criminal history variables only)	Predicted percentage reconvicted (criminal history and social variables)	Total number
Straight probation	52.7	51.3*	52.4	2712
Probation with requirements	57.6	54.7	55.2	455
CSO	42.7	44.6*	43.7*	3591
Combination order	53.4	50.9*	51.2*	684
All disposals	48.2	48.2	48.2	7442

Note: *Significantly different from actual rate.

Source: Adapted from May, 1999, p. 43.

that 37% of those discharged from custody had more than 11 previous convictions, compared to only 12% within the CPO group. As shown in Table 3.6, the lowest actual reconviction rate was for the CPO (38.1%), although the difference between the actual and predicted figures was not statistically significant.

A further re-offending study, based on a cohort in 2009, did not control for known differences in offender characteristics, making it difficult to assess the effectiveness of particular sentences (Ministry of Justice, 2011b). Crucially, it does provide reconviction rates separated by community order requirements. As shown in Table 3.7, the 'standalone' unpaid work requirement achieved the lowest reconviction rate (25.3%), followed by curfew and unpaid work (31.3%). However, offenders on these requirements had the lowest average number of previous offences (9.9 and 11.0 respectively), thus the variation in re-offending rates might be explained by differences in offender seriousness.

In summary, adult offenders on community service tend to achieve lower reconviction rates when compared to probation or custody. Crucially however, the more reliable studies indicate that this pattern remains when adjustment is made for the criminal history and social characteristics of offenders (Lloyd *et al.*, 1994; May, 1999; Spicer and Glicksman, 2004). Thus, it is argued that adult community service may

DOI: 10.1057/9781137400468.0007

TABLE 3.6   *Adult reconviction: results from the 2001 Cohort [%]*

Disposal	Number	Actual rate	Predicted rate	Difference
Community Rehabilitation Orders (Probation Centre/specified activities)	2,638	59.6	59.2	0.7
Community Rehabilitation Order (other)	9,319	60.0	61.1	−1.8
Community Punishment Order	**10,069**	**38.1**	**38.3**	**−0.5**
Community Punishment and Rehabilitation Order	3,636	53.3	53.9	−1.1
Drug Treatment and Testing Order	594	86.0	79.9	7.6*
Prison Discharges	14,569	58.2	60.1	−3.2*
All Offenders	40,825	53.7	54.7	−1.8*

Note: *Statistically significant

Source: Adapted from Spicer and Glicksman, 2004, p. 6.

TABLE 3.7   *Community orders detail: reconviction rates by requirement type, 2009 Cohort (requirements selected here are based on 100 or more offenders)*

Requirement	Number of offenders	Reconviction rate %	Average number of previous offences
Unpaid work	9,710	25.3	9.9
Supervision	3,377	42.1	22.6
Accredited programme and supervision	3,116	35.3	18.1
Unpaid work and supervision	2,200	33.5	14.0
Drug rehabilitation and supervision	1,513	66.4	40.1
Curfew	918	42.9	22.8
Specified activity and supervision	568	46.1	19.5
Curfew and unpaid work	508	31.3	11.0
Curfew and supervision	493	46.7	23.5
Accredited programme, drug rehabilitation and supervision	442	73.5	46.4
Alcohol treatment and supervision	425	44.5	19.7
Accredited programme and supervision	264	48.9	22.1
Accredited programme, specified activity and supervision	256	52.0	20.5
Specified activity, unpaid work and supervision	238	42.6	12.8

Continued

DOI: 10.1057/9781137400468.0007

TABLE 3.7   Continued

Requirement	Number of offenders	Reconviction rate %	Average number of previous offences
Specified activity and unpaid work	170	38.2	10.6
Curfew, unpaid work and supervision	162	46.3	16.9
Accredited programme, alcohol treatment and supervision	161	41.6	20.4
Drug rehabilitation	135	70.4	38.1
Drug rehabilitation, specified activity and supervision	131	71.8	33.6
Mental health and supervision	109	32.1	16.6
Alcohol treatment, unpaid work and supervision	102	41.2	11.1

Source: Adapted from Ministry of Justice, 2011b, pp. 32–33.

have a positive impact upon recidivism, a conclusion which has been noted by several academic researchers. For instance, Rex and Gelsthorpe (2002) have stated, *'could it be...that offenders undergo constructive and re-integrative experiences in undertaking community work'* (p. 316). Moreover, in response to the encouraging reconviction results outlined above, McIvor (2002, p. 10) posed the following question: *'What makes community service effective?'* The following section, therefore, aims to address this question, by drawing upon four key studies that have specifically explored offenders' experiences of the disposal.

Studies into adult community service

The key findings from the four main studies are summarised in Table 3.8. Unsurprisingly, evaluators have utilised different methodologies of varying quality. Certainly, it can be argued that most have limited sample sizes and there is a general lack of quantitative and qualitative data. Moreover, the partial findings are now dated, with the last study undertaken in England and Wales in 2001 (Rex *et al.*, 2003). Nonetheless, they provide a valuable contribution to the knowledge base relating to community service and they are discussed, in turn, further below.

DOI: 10.1057/9781137400468.0007

TABLE 3.8 *Summary of studies into adult community service*

Study	Sample size and offender profiles	Methodology	Summary of selected findings
Offenders on community service express their opinions in Warwickshire (Varah, 1981).	• 100 offenders. • No information on offender characteristics.	• Questionnaires completed after CS hours.	• 86% of offenders gained something positive from their CS experience, including: teamwork skills; satisfaction from helping others; decorating or bricklaying skills and full time employment. • 52% of offenders stated that CS could be improved in some way. • Offenders requested a greater variety of projects and they disliked menial unskilled tasks which had no perceived benefit (i.e. simple gardening or litter picking).
The operation and impact of community service by offenders in Scotland (McIvor, 1991, 1992).	• 406 offenders. • 95.6% male. • Average age 23.4 years. • Average of 5 previous convictions. • Dishonesty most common offence (55.9%), followed by violence (26.8%).	• Analysis of case records and 136 questionnaires.	• 72.5% of participants stated that they had gained something positive from their CS experience. • Offenders found the work: interesting (87.9%); enjoyable (91%); useful to beneficiaries (96%) and worthwhile (87.4%). Furthermore, 68.7% of offenders gained new skills. • 88% suggested that they would be willing to undertake community service on a voluntary basis in the future. • Actual reconviction rate of 40.3% within 12 months and 57.5% within 24 months. • Offenders who believed CS was worthwhile were less likely to be reconvicted than those who perceived the experience as insignificant.

DOI: 10.1057/9781137400468.0007

Study			
What's promising in community service? Implementation of seven pathfinder projects (Rex et al, 2003).	• 1851 offenders. • 92% male. • 89% white. • Average age 27. • Most common offence motoring (28%), followed by violence (23%).	• CRIME PICS 11 and 816 offender questionnaires. • Project hampered by lack of priority and staff commitment to Pathfinder scheme.	• 91% of respondents agreed that CS provided an opportunity to help others; 77% felt that it was a chance to learn new skills; 61% agreed that the sanction was good at keeping people out of trouble; 63% valued their placements. • Only 36% of offenders felt that CS improved their skills and 40% felt that the experience supported them in gaining employment. • 76% felt that CS reduced their likelihood of re-offending.
An evaluation of the community reparation pilots in Scotland (Curran et al., 2007).	• 70 offenders. • 87% male. • Average age 22. • 63% previous convictions. • Breach of the peace most common offence (54%).	• Analysis of CRO monitoring data. • Interviews with local authority staff; 10 Justices of the Peace; 4 Sheriffs and 17 offenders.	• Limited qualitative data. • 8 offenders (out of the 17 interviewed) enjoyed the work or specific elements; 8 participants undertook menial tasks and did not believe that they gained anything positive from the experience. • 16 respondents provided positive praise regarding their supervisors and there was evidence of pro-social modelling.

DOI: 10.1057/9781137400468.0007

In the early 1980s, Varah distributed 100 questionnaires within Warwickshire probation service, in order to explore adult offenders' opinions of community service. It is important to recognise from the outset that this study lacks important details and the author describes it as an 'unsophisticated' study which does not engage in detailed statistics or discussion (Varah, 1981, p. 121; see also Pease, 1985).

In general, the results were encouraging as 86 participants felt that they had gained something positive from their community service experience. Although limited, a breakdown of the available results indicate that 18 offenders had gained team-working skills; 13 had enhanced satisfaction from helping others; eight gained decorating or bricklaying skills; two offenders obtained full-time employment; two had an improved work ethic and six participants stated that they had increased self-confidence and a greater respect for people.

Participants were asked to compare their experience of community service to incarceration. Just over half (55) had experience of custody and 15 offenders argued that community service helped others, making a positive contribution. Moreover, 11 offenders supported the view of one participant, who stated that: *'Prison is negative, costly and destructive...whereas community service is positive, constructive and enhancing for society and offender alike* (cited in Varah, 1981, p. 122). This was an unusually articulate response to a leading question, thus it can be argued that questionnaire validity may have been affected by social desirability bias, whereby research participants conform to socially acceptable values (Robson, 2002; Johnson and Fendrich, 2005; King and Brunner, 2000; Huang *et al.*, 1998).

Offenders were also asked whether they disliked anything about community service and 52 offenders believed that it could be improved in some way, including more work for the elderly and better equipment. Most importantly, 17 offenders argued for a wider variety of tasks, in order to avoid menial unskilled activities, which had no perceived benefit. Nevertheless, 67% of offenders stated that they would be willing to return to community service on a voluntary basis, thus highlighting the re-integrative potential of the sanction (Varah, 1981, p. 123).

Ten years later, McIvor (1991, 1992) undertook a more comprehensive study of 12 community service schemes across four social work areas, involving 406 offenders within Scotland. The primary aim of this study was to examine the attitudes and responses of offenders to different types of work. Data regarding the sample and operation of the schemes was drawn from case file records and 136 offenders responded to a

DOI: 10.1057/9781137400468.0007

questionnaire upon completion of their hours (McIvor, 1991, p. 20; see also McIvor, 1992, p. 19).

Of most interest to this current study are McIvor's results from questionnaires. In general, the findings were positive as 87.4% of participants felt that their community service was worthwhile and 72.5% thought that they had gained something positive from the experience. In particular, offenders found the work interesting (87.9%) and enjoyable (91%), with 74.6% utilising existing skills or 68.7% learning new skills (either practical or interpersonal). In addition, 91.1% enjoyed contact with beneficiaries and 96.3% felt that the work undertaken would benefit them. Similar to Varah's (1981) earlier study, 88% of offenders stated that they would be willing to undertake community service on a voluntary basis in the future, once again demonstrating the re-integrative potential of the disposal[2] (McIvor, 1991, p. 24; 1992, p. 84).

Offender attitudes, however, varied greatly depending upon their placement experiences. As shown in Table 3.9, offenders found community service significantly more interesting, enjoyable and worthwhile if

TABLE 3.9   *Offenders' attitudes and contact with beneficiaries (acquisition of skills and usefulness of work)*

Contact with beneficiaries		
Offenders' attitudes	**A great deal**	**Some/None**
Very interesting**	53.2%	19.2%
Very enjoyable**	49.3%	20.8%
Very worthwhile*	62.3%	40.4%
Acquisition of skills *(practical or interpersonal)*		
Offenders' attitudes	**A great deal**	**Some/None**
Very interesting**	68%	30.8%
Very enjoyable**	64%	31.5%
Very worthwhile**	84%	45.8%
How useful		
Offenders' attitudes	**Very**	**Fairly/not at all**
Very interesting***	48.9%	17.8%
Very enjoyable**	48.3%	17.8%
Very worthwhile***	65.2%	29.5%
Willing to be placed on CS again**	94.3%	75%

Notes: * = $p < 0.05$: ** = $p < 0.01$; *** = $p < 0.001$.

Source: Adapted from McIvor, 1992, pp. 87–88.

DOI: 10.1057/9781137400468.0007

they were able to attain new skills during their placements; have direct contact with beneficiaries (entailing a level of reciprocity or exchange) and engage in meaningful work perceived as useful to recipients (see McIvor, 1991, p. 26; McIvor, 2002, p. 2).

Within the questionnaire, McIvor (1991) also asked offenders to indicate their likelihood of further offending. Of the 97 participants who completed the question, 72.9% stated that they were *unlikely* to commit further offences and 18.8% felt that it was *fairly likely* that they would re-offend. Crucially, those offenders that had gained something positive from their work, such as employability skills, were *less likely* to predict that they would re-offend, when compared to those who gained nothing (20.7% vs. 41.2%) (McIvor, 1992, p. 153).

It is widely acknowledged that prediction of recidivism by offenders is unreliable, due to distortions in their self perception (Bottomley and Pease, 1993; Jupp, Davies and Francis, 2000; Bryman, 2001; Holt and Pamment, 2011). Thus, McIvor (1992) recorded actual reconviction rates for 136 offenders, in which 40.3% were reconvicted within 12 months and 57.5% within 24 months. Interestingly, offenders that believed their community service was *worthwhile* had fewer new convictions (2.9 vs. 4.6) and they were *less likely* to be reconvicted than those who perceived the experience as meaningless (56.9% vs. 70.5%) (McIvor, 1992, p. 169; McIvor, 2002, p. 2). However, with such small numbers in the reconviction sample, the findings should be treated with caution.

In response to McIvor's (1991, 1992) earlier research outlined above and other studies suggesting that the disposal may reduce recidivism (Lloyd *et al.*, 1994; Raynor and Vanstone, 1996; May, 1999), seven community service 'Pathfinder' projects were introduced. The aim was to examine positive approaches within the disposal that could reduce re-offending, including pro-social modelling (PSM); skills accreditation and tackling other offending-related needs (TON) (Rex *et al.*, 2003; Gelsthorpe and Rex, 2004).

It is important to note here, that the initiative suffered greatly from a lack of priority and focus, right from its inception. According to probation staff, this was due to limited commitment, confusion relating to best practice, unclear study aims and objectives and concern for the overall feasibility of the project (Rex *et al.*, 2003, p. 33). Therefore, the mixed results outlined below could be due to poor project delivery and implementation failure.

The study utilised a sample of 1,851 offenders and it drew upon probation area databases; supervision records; Offenders Index (Home Office

DOI: 10.1057/9781137400468.0007

database of convictions); assessment forms and termination summaries completed by staff; interviews with 127 members of staff; CRIME PICS 11 (a measurement of offender attitudes, see Frude, Honess and Maguire, 1994) and 816 offender questionnaires. However, a reconviction study was not undertaken (Rex *et al.*, 2003; Gelsthorpe and Rex, 2004).

Results show that only 54% of offenders gained accredited awards, but the reasons for this remain unclear. Nonetheless, 73% successfully completed their ordered hours and data from CRIME PICS 11 demonstrated statistically significant reductions in pro-criminal attitudes (−1.0) and self-perceived problems (−0.8) (Rex *et al.*, 2003, p. 4). Whilst these results are encouraging, it can be argued that offenders completing the test on two occasions were more likely to show positive change than those who did not participate. Thus, the results are perhaps unrepresentative of the sample and the positive findings may not be a consequence of the community service intervention.

Of most interest to this current study are the results from offender questionnaires completed within the last 20 hours of their community service. In total, questionnaires from 44 % of the sample were obtained, representing 61% of those who successfully completed their orders. As shown in Table 3.10, offenders held positive views about community service as a sentence. In particular, participants agreed that it provided an opportunity to help others (91%), 77% felt that it was a chance to learn new skills and 61% agreed that the sanction was good at keeping people 'out of trouble' (Rex *et al.*, 2003, p. 61).

Offenders were also asked whether community service made a positive personal 'difference' and as shown in Table 3.11, the results were

TABLE 3.10   *Views on community service as a sentence, by order type*

Views on CS as a sentence	CPOs agreeing (n=609)	COs agreeing (n=182)	Overall agreeing (n=791)
A chance to do something for other people	90%	93%	91%
A chance to learn new skills	76%	82%	77%
Good at keeping people out of trouble	61%	62%	61%
Better than going to prison	96%	96%	96%
A fair sentence for me	77%	80%	78%

Source: Adapted from Rex *et al.*, 2003, p. 61.

DOI: 10.1057/9781137400468.0007

TABLE 3.11   *Views on community service impact*

	CS improved skills a lot/quite a lot	Quite likely to do more training	CS will help to get a new job
Total (n=789)	36%	34%	40%

	Changed the way I see things (attitudes)	Changed the way I behave	Make me less likely to offend
Total (n=786)	58%	47%	76%

Source: Adapted from Rex *et al.*, 2003, pp. 63–64.

less encouraging. Whilst there is limited information on the placement activities undertaken, only 36% of offenders felt that community service improved their skills and 40% felt that the experience supported them in gaining employment. Despite these relatively low scores, 76% felt that community service reduced their likelihood of re-offending. Crucially however, the authors found no association between type of Pathfinder project (PSM, SA or TON) and subsequent offenders' views on the impact of community service (Rex *et al.*, 2003, p. 63).

Three months after completion of their community service hours, follow-up questionnaires were received from 267 offenders, in order to check participants' employment status and to ask whether they had received a new charge or court appearance. Of the respondents, 84% had no further charge or court appearance and 59% reported being in full time work, with 36% experiencing a positive change in employment status. Crucially however, only 17% attributed this to their time on community service. Whilst these findings remain useful, the results must be interpreted with caution, as it can be argued that follow-up questionnaires were received from more compliant participants. Moreover, in the absence of a comprehensive reconviction study, the results are unreliable (Rex *et al.*, 2003, p. 4).

The Pathfinder project was the last study to explore the re-integrative and rehabilitative potential of community service within England and Wales. However, in 2007, Curran *et al.* undertook an evaluation into Community Reparation Orders[3] (CROs) on behalf of the Scottish Executive. It is important to note here, that CROs differ from YJ Reparation Orders within England and Wales, as they are specifically designed to tackle anti-social behaviour and they are available for adult offenders (Curran *et al.*, 2007).

DOI: 10.1057/9781137400468.0007

Of most relevance to this current study are the 17 interviews under-taken with offenders,[4] in order to examine the impact of CROs (see Curran *et al.*, 2007, p. 59). These offenders represented a very small compliant 'subgroup', thus the reliability of the findings should be treated with caution. Additionally, the qualitative results are extremely limited as according to the evaluators, focused information was difficult to obtain from offenders (Curran *et al.*, 2007, p. 59).

During the interviews, offenders were asked whether they had a posi-tive or negative experience of community service. Eight participants stated that they enjoyed the work undertaken on community service. For instance, one offender stated, '*I liked getting rid of graffiti because it made the area look better*'. Conversely, eight offenders believed that they had not gained anything positive from the experience. Crucially for this current study, the work undertaken by these offenders was of a menial nature and included litter picking, sweeping leaves and general clearance work (Curran *et al.*, 2007, p. 64).

Interestingly, 16 offenders offered positive praise regarding their supervisors and according to the evaluators, there was evidence of pro-social modelling (Curran *et al.*, 2007, p. 66). In particular, participants suggested that they had been treated fairly and with respect and there was evidence that supervisors had accommodated the needs of partici-pants. For instance, Curran *et al.* (2007) cite one example, whereby an offender was pleased with the additional drug support and advice that a supervisor had provided (p. 66).

Offenders were also asked whether they had committed offences since commencing their CRO. Ten participants (59%) stated that they had broken the law but unsurprisingly, there was a reluctance to discuss and divulge details. Of this group, six were 'optimistic' that this would not happen again. A reconviction study was not undertaken and given the limited timescale and potential compliance bias within the sample, this data should be treated as highly unreliable (Curran *et al.*, 2007, p. 73).

Taken together, the key findings outlined above indicate that adult offenders *can* find community service beneficial, specifically through the completion of worthwhile work and the acquisition of employability skills, which can lead to reductions in re-offending (McIvor, 1992; McIvor, 2002). However, the studies highlight the important link between the quality of the work undertaken and the perceived value of the experi-ence. In particular, offenders should be given a variety of meaningful placements where they can acquire new skills, maximise contact with

DOI: 10.1057/9781137400468.0007

beneficiaries and the activities should be perceived as useful to recipients (Varah, 1981; McIvor, 1991; Rex *et al.*, 2003; Curran *et al.*, 2007). The following section now turns to examining reconviction results relating to the youth justice Reparation Order, before outlining the few studies which have investigated the impact of community reparation on young offenders. It then integrates the research evidence base for both adult community service and youth justice community reparation.

Youth justice community reparation: reconviction results

As previously noted, youth justice community reparation has a much shorter history, having been introduced within the Reparation Order, under the Crime and Disorder Act 1998. Thus, there are far fewer reconviction studies to draw upon. However, shortly after Youth Offending Teams (YOTs) were implemented throughout England and Wales, Jennings (2003) undertook a one year reconviction study into youth justice community interventions, with a sample of 20,926 male offenders. Utilising logistic regression to control for offender seriousness, a predicted rate of reconviction was calculated, based upon a cohort tracked in 1997 with similar characteristics (see Jennings, 2003, p. 8; McNeill, 2006). Reconviction rates by disposal type are presented in Table 3.12.

Although several commentators have been critical of this study, arguing that there is ambiguity in utilising an 'adjusted predicted' baseline (see Bateman and Pitts, 2005; Bottoms and Dignan, 2004; McNeill, 2006), the results do show that the Reparation Order achieved a reconviction rate of 51.2%, lower than expected (59%), when considering age, length of criminal career and previous cautions and/or convictions. In fact, as Jennings (2003) acknowledged, this was the lowest rate of any court disposal (p. 8), once again indicating that unpaid work may have a positive impact upon offenders.

Despite the criticisms of Jennings (2003), later reconviction studies undertaken within youth justice have not controlled for variations in offender characteristics or other factors affecting re-offending or type of sentence given (Ministry of Justice, 2011a, p. 15). Moreover, a predicted rate of reconviction could not be calculated for the Reparation Order over an eight-year period from 2000 to 2008, due to unspecified 'problems' with archived data (see Ministry of Justice, 2011a, p. 27). It is, therefore, impossible

DOI: 10.1057/9781137400468.0007

TABLE 3.12   *Reconviction rates by community disposal for males in 2001*

Disposal	Actual reconviction rate	Adjusted predicted reconviction rate (1997 rate adjusted to 2001 characteristics)	+/– Change	Numbers
Action Plan	53.7	60.2	–6.5	795
Attendance Order	62.6	61.4	+1.2	631
Community rehabilitation	70.4	68.6	+1.8	108
Conditional discharge	50.9	57.4	–6.5	804
Fine	51.3	59.4	–8.1	863
Reparation order	**51.2**	**59.0**	**–7.8**	**869**
Reprimand	13.0	24.5	–11.5	9,599
Supervision order	67.8	68.5	–0.7	742
Final warning	30.2	36.5	–6.3	5,361
Other	63.7	62.3	+1.4	402
All court disposals	57.4	61.1	–3.7	5,899
Overall males	30.0	37.9	–7.9	20,926

Source: Adapted from Jennings, 2003, p. 14.

to adequately compare the effectiveness of youth justice disposals (Jennings, 2003; Ministry of Justice, 2011a; Whiting and Cuppleditch, 2006).

Crucially, it is important to note here, that re-offending rates do reveal decreasing effectiveness over time with regards to the Reparation Order. Data supplied by the Ministry of Justice (2011a), shows an increase in re-offending rates for the Reparation Order, from 54.2% in 2002 to 67.2% in 2009. This is only marginally lower than the extremely high re-offending rate achieved by incarceration (see also Whiting and Cuppleditch, 2006). The reasons for this increase in re-offending rates, over this seven-year period, remain unclear (Whiting and Cuppleditch, 2006; Ministry of Justice, 2011a). However, the following section discusses the findings of four studies which have briefly explored the impact of community reparation on young offenders.

Studies into youth justice community reparation

The relevant findings from the four studies are summarised in Table 3.13. Most importantly, these studies have only touched on the effectiveness

TABLE 3.13 Summary of studies into youth justice community reparation

Study	Sample size and offender profiles	Methodology	Summary of selected findings
National evaluation of the pilot Youth Offending Teams (Holdaway et al., 2001).	• 602 reparation orders. • 85% male. • Mean age 14.3 (range 10–18). • 62% in school or further education. • 52% had one or two minor convictions. • Theft/dishonesty most common offence (48%).	• Analysis of case files. • Case study interview data with offender, staff and parents. • Sentencing statistics. • Data collection varied by each YOT and record keeping considered 'poor'.	• Community reparation most common intervention. • Offenders did not understand the order. • Offenders given limited range of activities. • Little connection between work and offender/offence.
National evaluation of the YJB's RJ projects (Wilcox and Hoyle, 2004).	• Data available for 42 RJ projects, 6800 offenders. • 76% male. • Age range 14–17. • 90% white. • Theft most common offence (30%), followed by violence (23%). • Offenders in 'early stages of criminal career'.	• Questionnaires for victims and offenders. • Significant variation in methodologies adopted by 'local' evaluators. • 1/3 of projects unable to provide basic data.	• Over-reliance on community reparation. • Primarily perceived as a punishment by offenders with no clear benefit to victims or community. • Placements not relevant to crimes committed.
'Local' evaluation of an RJ project in the South West of England (Gray et al., 2003; Gray, 2005).	• 214 young offenders. • 81.3% male. • Average age 14.5 years (range 10–18). • 96.1% white. • Theft most common offence (37.8%). • 78.3% no previous convictions.	• Quantitative data obtained from YOT's own database and ASSET. • Interviews with 41 offenders and 21 victims.	• Primarily perceived as a punishment by offenders, in place to deter future offending. • Community reparation unfair to victims. • Offenders disappointed that they could not make amends directly.
Evaluation of the Intensive Supervision and Surveillance Programme (ISSP) (Gray et al., 2005).	• 3,384 ISSP cases recorded. • 93% male. • Mean age 16.4 years. • 83.5% white. • Average of nine previous offences. • Burglary most common offence (24.7%).	• Qualitative data: Interviews with 173 offenders; 144 staff and 33 parents.	• Offenders unable to relate to menial tasks, including litter picking and leafleting. • Activities with a lack of purpose considered 'pointless' and a waste of time'.

DOI: 10.1057/9781137400468.0007

of community reparation as part of wider ranging evaluations of youth justice sanctions. Thus, they contain a distinct lack of data relating specifically to the intervention. Additionally, several of the reports were written for the Home Office or YOT management and the varying methodologies and numbers involved remain imprecise, resulting in limited and descriptive analyses (Holdaway *et al.*, 2001; Wilcox and Hoyle, 2004). Nonetheless, they are discussed, in turn, further below.

In 2001, Holdaway *et al.* published an assessment of the pilot YOTs in West London; Sheffield; Wessex and Wolverhampton. Of most significance to this current study, is the brief examination that was undertaken into the court orders introduced within the CDA 1998, including reparation. In particular, data was collected regarding 602 reparation orders, of which 85% were male and they had a mean age of 14.3 years (ranging from 10 to 18). The majority of offenders (52%) had one or two previous convictions and these were for relatively minor offences such as theft and dishonesty (48%) (Holdaway *et al.*, 2001, p. 89).

According to Holdaway *et al.* (2001, p. 91), young people on community reparation were given a very limited range of menial tasks to complete, consisting primarily of 'unchallenging' gardening or shrub clearance work. Moreover, there was little correlation between the tasks, offender and offence. During interviews with YOT staff, supervisors acknowledged the difficulty in establishing adequate numbers of 'quality placements', although the reasons for this remain unclear. However, as the researchers indicate, it would appear that the implementation of general 'unskilled' tasks were far easier to organise than meaningful placements, capable of facilitating the acquisition of skills (Holdaway *et al.*, 2001, p. 91).

Holdaway *et al.* (2001) warned that community reparation was degenerating into a 'tokenistic response', whereby offenders gain little from the process (p. 38). It was concluded that young people on the intervention should be allocated to a range of engaging activities which are closely linked to the offence, allowing them to see the connection. Most importantly, tasks should relate to the interests of offenders and develop new skills, which can lead to reductions in re-offending (McGuire, 1995; Farrall, 2002; Hollin and Palmer, 2006).

Three years later, the YJB funded an assessment of 46 restorative justice interventions. Despite substantial variation in the methodologies adopted by 'local' evaluators and a lack of information provided by a third of projects, 'generic' data was available for 42 schemes. These

DOI: 10.1057/9781137400468.0007

worked with 6,800 offenders, of which 76% were male, aged 14 to 17 years (80%) and theft was the most common offence (30%) leading to referral, followed by violence (23%). According to Wilcox and Hoyle (2004, p. 5), offenders were within the 'early stages of their criminal career'.

In response to growing concerns at the time regarding the quality of community reparation, possibly due to the negative results outlined above (Holdaway *et al.*, 2001), *Crime Concern* (then national supporters of the approach) provided the evaluators with guidelines regarding 'best practice'. Although it is difficult to establish the origin of these guidelines, it was stated that placements should: relate to the offence; develop or enhance young persons' skills and interests; encourage offenders to consider the consequences of their actions on victims and the community and address issues such as unstructured / unsupervised leisure time (*Crime Concern* cited by Wilcox and Hoyle, 2004, p. 35).

The evaluators state that only four projects (out of a possible 42) adhered to the good practice guidelines provided by *Crime Concern* (Wilcox and Hoyle, 2004, p. 35). Although there were 'several' examples of positive placement provision, including the restoration of prosthetic limbs for landmine victims, results were described as 'unfavourable'. In particular, it was discovered that offenders were being allocated to a limited range of menial activities, which were primarily perceived as a punishment by offenders and of no value to victims or the wider community. Furthermore, the tasks were not relevant to the crimes committed. Recognising the potential of community reparation as a creative disposal, Wilcox and Hoyle (2004, p. 35) stressed the importance of engaging placements, facilitating skills acquisition.

As part of the national evaluation, Wilcox and Hoyle (2004, p. 44) undertook a small reconviction study, providing a breakdown by intervention type, utilising data from the Police National Computer (PNC). Table 3.14 shows the results from 34 restorative justice projects and they relate to young offenders sentenced between July and September 2000, with a follow up period of 12 months. The community reparation ('partly restorative') cohort achieved a reconviction rate of 47.3%. This was below the reconviction rate achieved by the 'mostly restorative' interventions of indirect mediation and direct reparation (52.4 % and 47.6% respectively).

There were however, a number of problems regarding the quality of the PNC data utilised within this reconviction study and the original sample size (n=827) was substantially reduced (see Wilcox and Hoyle,

DOI: 10.1057/9781137400468.0007

TABLE 3.14   *Reconviction rate by type of restorative intervention (34 projects)*

Restorative intervention	Number in sample	% of sample	% reconvicted
Direct meeting (fully restorative)	89	12.2	41.6
Indirect mediation (mostly restorative)	42	5.8	52.4
Direct reparation (mostly restorative)	145	19.9	47.6
Community reparation (partly restorative)	201	27.6	47.3
Victim awareness (partly restorative)	126	17.3	42.1
Other	21	2.9	66.7
Not known	103	14.2	47.6

Source: Adapted from Wilcox and Hoyle, 2004, p. 48.

2004, p. 44). Due to the small numbers involved, it is therefore impossible to make appropriate comparisons between projects. Furthermore, age; gender and criminal history were not controlled for. Although it provides a useful but somewhat tentative indication of reconviction by intervention type, the results should be treated as unreliable.

As part of the national study of restorative justice interventions outlined above (Wilcox and Hoyle, 2004), Gray *et al.* (2003; Gray, 2005) published a 'local' evaluation of projects developed by a YOT in the south west of England. Of most interest to this research are the extremely limited and negative qualitative findings that emerged from 41 offender interviews (Gray, 2005, p. 942).

Although there is no information on the placement activities provided, offenders who undertook community reparation perceived no personal benefit from the disposal. Instead, they viewed its primary purpose as punishment which is in place to deter further offending. Young offenders were also concerned regarding the unfairness of community reparation to the victim, and the fact that they were unable to make amends directly (Gray, 2005, p. 945).

Later research into the effectiveness of the Intensive Supervision and Surveillance Programme (ISSP) for severe and persistent offenders, also briefly explored the impact of community reparation upon young offenders (see Gray *et al.*, 2005; Ellis, Pamment and Lewis, 2009). As part of the qualitative study, Gray *et al.* (2005) interviewed 173 young people, 144 staff and 33 parents.

According to the researchers, young people who undertook community reparation completed a range of projects including gardening, recycling and environmental improvements. Crucially however, offenders preferred being involved in constructive and engaging activities where they could work with other people and develop new skills. For instance, one young person stated: '*We've done gardening and DIY stuff; it's taught me how to do things I haven't done before.*' Conversely, offenders were unable to relate to menial activities such as litter picking; shrub clearance and leafleting, describing them as a '*waste of time*' and '*boring*'. Therefore, Gray *et al.* (2005, p. 118) concluded by warning against the utilisation of 'pointless' and non-stimulating placements, which lack direct purpose.

Overall, the limited findings outlined above indicate that YOTs are providing young people with a narrow range of menial placements, such as unskilled shrub clearance or litter picking. Furthermore, there is little correlation between the work undertaken and the offender or offence, consequently the disposal is perceived as a punishment, with little benefit to the young person or wider community. The final section below provides a brief review of the key themes identified within this chapter.

Review

This chapter has shown that reconviction rates relating to adult community service are consistently lower than predicted when considering the criminal history and social characteristics of offenders (Lloyd *et al.*, 1994; May, 1999; Spicer and Glicksman, 2004). This positive pattern has remained for 30 years, thus highlighting the possibility that the disposal has a beneficial impact upon offenders (McIvor, 2002; Rex and Gelsthorpe, 2002). Certainly, additional research supports this reconviction trend, with evidence of associated positive practice relating to the supervision of community service (Varah, 1981; McIvor, 1991, 1992; Rex *et al.*, 2003).

Conversely, reconviction rates for the youth justice reparation order have been steadily increasing since 2000, demonstrating declining effectiveness. Alongside this data, available research evidence shows that youth justice community reparation is not being operated effectively by YOTs (Holdaway *et al.*, 2001; Wilcox and Hoyle, 2004; Gray, *et al.*, 2005).

The research evidence base for adult community service and youth justice community reparation is integrated in Table 3.15. It is clear that

DOI: 10.1057/9781137400468.0007

TABLE 3.15 *Summary and integration of positive and negative practices relating to unpaid work (YJCR and adult CS) most likely to lead to successful outcomes*

Positive unpaid work	Negative unpaid work	Research evidence from adult community service and youth justice community reparation
Offenders undertake a variety of **meaningful tasks** related to original offences.	Offenders undertake a **narrow range of menial** work placements and there is an **overreliance on shrub clearance / litter picking.**	Varah (1981); McIvor, (1991, 1992); Holdaway *et al.* (2001); Wilcox and Hoyle (2004); Rex *et al.*, (2003); Curran *et al.* (2007).
Tasks enable offenders to **gain or utilise existing skills.** Placements involve a level of **problem solving, stimulation and challenge.** Placements encourage a **constructive working relationship** between offenders and staff, adopting a pro-social modelling approach.	Offenders are provided with basic placements. The work requires **limited engagement and problem solving. No attainment of skills.** Work in this category can be characterised as merely **'tokenistic'.**	Varah (1981); McIvor, (1991, 1992); Holdaway *et al.* (2001); Rex *et al.*, (2003); Wilcox and Hoyle (2004); Curran *et al.* (2007).
Placements **maximise contact with beneficiaries,** requiring a level of reciprocity and exchange. Work perceived by offenders as **worthwhile and useful** to beneficiaries/community.	Offenders have **no contact with beneficiaries.** Work placements primarily perceived by offenders as punishment.	McIvor (1991, 1992); Gray (2005); Gray *et al.* (2005); Holdaway *et al.* (2001). McIvor (1991, 1992); Rex (2003); Wilcox and Hoyle (2004); Gray (2005); Gray *et al.* (2005); Curran *et al.* (2007).
Staff members are committed to the **re-integrative and rehabilitative** potential of unpaid work.	**Staff members are not committed** to unpaid work and perceive its primary purpose as **punishment.**	Rex *et al.* (2003); Curran *et al.* (2007).

DOI: 10.1057/9781137400468.0007

in order for unpaid work to have a beneficial impact upon offenders, a number of key elements must be in place. In particular, offenders must undertake a variety of constructive tasks and they must gain or utilise existing skills, through activities that are perceived as useful to beneficiaries.

It is important to note here, that within a youth justice context, there are currently no evidence-based guidelines on the effective delivery of youth justice community reparation, leading to reductions in reoffending. Indeed, the YJB have been criticised for not adhering to an evidenced-based approach (Kogan, 1999; Goldson, 2001; Nutley, Davies and Tilley, 2000). Crucially, guidance provided to YOTs by the YJB on how to develop reparation, as part of the Youth Crime Action Plan, focuses on improving the visibility of the disposal, rather than outlining key elements of supervision most likely to lead to successful outcomes (YJB, 2008). Therefore, there is certainly a need to develop an evidence-based best practice model using the criteria outlined above.

A further important finding to emerge from this chapter is that there is a lack of high quality research into unpaid work for offenders (McIvor, 1993; Schiff, 1999; Hazel, Hagell and Brazier, 2002; Rex and Gelsthorpe, 2002; McGagh, 2007). Indeed, there are only a few notable studies which have explored adult offenders on community service and these are now somewhat dated (McIvor, 1991, 1993; Rex *et al.*, 2003). Moreover, within a youth justice context, there has been no research explicitly focusing upon community reparation. Instead, this chapter has had to focus upon large scale national evaluations of wider ranging youth justice sanctions, which have only briefly examined community reparation (Holdaway *et al.*, 2001; Wilcox and Hoyle, 2004; Gray *et al.*, 2005).

Therefore, it was essential to integrate the findings from adult studies with sparser information relating to young offenders. Whilst these youth justice studies are important, they reveal little about young offenders' perceptions of community reparation, their attitudes towards different types of work and the processes that actually take place during the disposal (Hazel, Hagell and Brazier, 2002; Rex and Gelsthorpe, 2002). Certainly, as shown above, young offenders' views have been neglected but as Delens-Ravier (2003, p. 164) has stressed, the impact of community reparation can only be understood in terms of what the young offender experiences.

There could be several reasons for the lack of research into YJ community reparation within England and Wales. As shown within the previous chapter, the paucity of research could be due to the lack of priority historically afforded to unpaid work (Ellis *et al.*, 1996; Rex and Gelsthorpe, 2002). Furthermore, Delens-Ravier (2003, p. 156) argues that it is extremely difficult to gain access to young offenders during and after their community reparation. Indeed, this gap in knowledge was a key motivation for this book and as a reparation supervisor with over six years' experience, the author was in a unique position to undertake research into young offenders' perceptions of community reparation.

Notes

1   See instead Lloyd, Mair and Hough (1994); Kershaw (1999); Goldblatt and Lewis (1998).
2   In a study of placement providers (see McIvor, 1993), it was discovered that approximately half of all agencies surveyed indicated that offenders had remained working in a voluntary or paid capacity after completion of their community service hours.
3   Introduced in May 2005 under the Anti-Social Behaviour etc (Scotland) Act 2004.
4   A further 22 interviews were organised but the offenders did not attend.

DOI: 10.1057/9781137400468.0007

4
Youth Justice Community Reparation in Practice

Abstract: *This chapter presents the results of the primary research study and due to the multi-methods design, it integrates the findings from both the quantitative and qualitative methods used. The secondary data obtained from Youth Offending Team (YOT) case files is presented first, followed by the primary data obtained from participant observation, assisted questionnaires and semi-structured interviews. Key themes covered include participants' perceptions of skills acquisition; problem solving; punishment; benefits for the community; reparation and attitudes towards re-offending. It uncovers serious inadequacies and failings regarding the organisation and delivery of the disposal.*

Pamment, Nicholas. *Community Reparation for Young Offenders: Perceptions, Policy and Practice.* Basingstoke: Palgrave Macmillan, 2016.
DOI: 10.1057/9781137400468.0008.

Secondary data: YOT case files

Of the 97 young offenders who participated in this study, most were male (74%), with an average age of 15.6 years (Figure 4.1). As shown in Figure 4.2, the majority of offenders were subject to Referral Orders (67%), followed by Reparation Orders (20%) and ISSPs (8%). Actual Bodily Harm (ABH) was the most common crime for which young offenders were referred (24%), followed by theft (21.9%) and drugs possession (9.4%) (see Figure 4.3). These offender characteristics are broadly similar to those found within the national restorative justice evaluations, discussed in Chapter 3 (Holdaway *et al.*, 2001; Wilcox and Hoyle, 2004; Gray *et al.*, 2005).

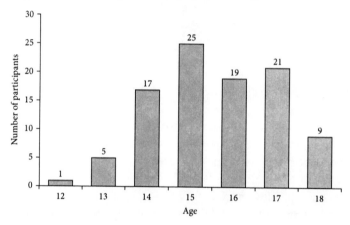

FIGURE 4.1   *Age of participants*

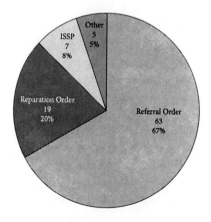

FIGURE 4.2   *Referral point*

DOI: 10.1057/9781137400468.0008

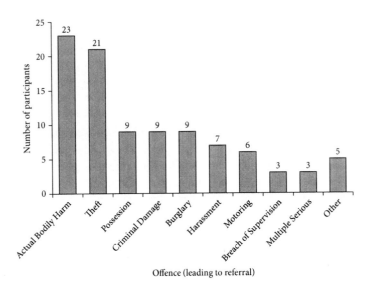

FIGURE 4.3   *Offence leading to referral*

Due to negotiated and restricted case file access, it was not possible to obtain comprehensive data relating to offending histories, such as number of previous convictions or prior experience of custody. Nonetheless, *Asset* scores reveal that participants were within the 'medium' risk category of re-offending, with a mean score of 13 (see also Baker, Jones, Roberts and Merrington, 2002, p. 7; Gray, 2005; Baker, 2004). It is important to note here, that a reconviction analysis was not possible due to a limited sample size, lack of comparison group and the need for 12–24-month data collection points from the completion of each offender's community disposal (see minimum standards for reconviction studies: YJB, 2008, p. 21; Home Office, 2004). In addition, breach information supplied by the YOT was incomplete, making a comprehensive analysis unfeasible: a problem experienced by other academic researchers within youth justice (Holdaway *et al.*, 2001; Wilcox and Hoyle, 2004).

Types of community reparation placement

The average length of community reparation placement was 14.7 hours and due to a lack of comparable data, it remains unclear how this relates to the national picture. As shown in Table 4.1, participants undertook a

DOI: 10.1057/9781137400468.0008

TABLE 4.1   *Placement type by non-skills and skills-based activities*

Non-skills based	n	Skills based	n
Shrub clearance	57	Painting and decorating	11
Litter picking	9	Fencing	5
'Kindling preparation'	8	Cementing	4
	74	Bird box making	2
	76.3	Bricklaying	1
Total		Total	23
Total % of sample		Total % of sample	23.7

narrow range of activities. Indeed, over half of all young people (58%) completed menial shrub clearance work, followed by painting and decorating (11%); litter picking (9%) and 'kindling preparation' (8%). Certainly, throughout the observation and supervisory period of two and a half years, there was an over-reliance on ground clearance work, with relatively little variation in placement allocation.

This represents a highly significant but negative early finding. The research evidence base relating to unpaid work (Chapter 3) shows the importance of providing offenders with a variety of meaningful tasks. These should closely relate to original offences and offenders, thus encouraging a greater consideration of the consequences of criminal behaviour (McIvor, 1991; Holdaway *et al.*, 2001; Wilcox and Hoyle, 2004; Gray *et al.*, 2005). However, these results suggest that the YOT has adopted a formulaic approach to workplace provision and there is an over-reliance on menial tasks. Most importantly, this strategy has been shown to prevent the acquisition of employability skills (Varah, 1981; Curran *et al.*, 2007). The overall picture was that only 23.7% ($n = 23$) of participants carried out 'meaningful' skills-based work.

Acquisition of employability skills

Having established the low skills content of over three quarters of YJCR placements, it was important to establish whether offenders were aware of this. Within the assisted questionnaire,[1] young offenders were asked to respond to the following statement: '*community reparation has given me new skills*'. Crucially, there was a statistically significant difference in mean scores between placement types. Offenders given menial tasks provided an extremely negative **mean** score of 1.8, whereas those given

DOI: 10.1057/9781137400468.0008

skills-based placements responded with a significantly higher **mean** score of **6.3** (i.e. close to the maximum score of 7, *strongly agree* on the Likert scale) $t\,(74.42) = -17.49$, $p < .001$. It is important to note here, that age and gender differences were also investigated. However, the sample was not large enough to show discernable differences and the similarity of tasks given to both male and female offenders within the narrow age band of the sample rendered this unsuitable for further analysis.

Qualitative analysis further supports these findings. Over half of all respondents given menial tasks ($n = 63$) argued that the basic nature of the activities prevented the attainment of employability skills. It is important to note here, that offenders' responses demonstrated a high degree of anger and frustration. Typical comments made by the young people are cited below:

> *Are you taking the piss? It's just clearing up; you don't get any skills from that.* (Young person/Male)
>
> *Clearing rubbish and driving it to the tip is hardly rocket science.* (Young person/ Male)
>
> *It's just pointless and a waste of time. How do you get skills from litter picking? Its crap.* (Young person/Female)

Conversely, offenders given skills-based placements ($n = 23$) responded more positively and the difference is stark here. Ten of these suggested that they had gained skills through the utilisation of tools. For example, one respondent had never used a drill prior to community reparation and they stated:

> *I have never used a drill like that before. I reckon I could use it again, on my own without any help.* (Young person/Male)

In addition, as shown in table 4.2 participants (9.3%) believed that they had learnt skills through painting or decorating and 5 (5.2%) felt that they had gained proficiency in fencing. Furthermore, 4 young people (4.1%) stated that they learnt how to mix cement and three respondents (3.1%) suggested that they could design and build bird boxes. During assisted questionnaire completion, it was apparent that these offenders were far less frustrated at their placements and this is encapsulated in the following comment:

> *I am well chuffed, I reckon I can put fences in on my own; was well hard but a decent thing to do.* (Young person/Male)

TABLE 4.2   *Offenders' qualitative responses to the acquisition of skills*

Skills gained	Number of participants	% of sample
None	63	64.9
'Using tools'	10	10.3
Painting and decorating	9	9.3
Fencing	5	5.2
Cementing	4	4.1
Design	3	3.1
Employment preparation	2	2.1
Working with others	1	1.0
Total	97	100

Throughout the observation and supervisory period, the most successful placement for skills learning appeared to be the installation of a concrete disabled ramp. Over a period of two days, four young people were required to mix cement to the correct consistency, lay the foundations and establish the correct gradient, requiring patience and basic mathematics. These offenders were extremely positive about their experience and two of the participants stated that the project had encouraged them to pursue a career in the building industry. For instance, one young person stated:

> *That was cool; I wouldn't mind doing this for a job. My Dad's a builder and I could go and work for him.* (Young person/Male)

As evidenced by the qualitative responses of offenders above, such a skills-orientated placement was extremely rare. Nonetheless, as shown below, it was clear that offenders recognised the importance of skills learning for future employability and desistance from crime:

> *Without qualifications and life skills, you're pretty much fucked.* (Young person/Male)

During staff interviews, supervisors were also asked to respond to whether: '*community reparation has given offenders new skills*' and they gave a near neutral **mean** score of **3.9**. Qualitative data reveals why this is near the neutral score of 4. All 12 members of staff argued that community reparation *could* facilitate skills learning but it is entirely dependent on the type of placements provided. Demonstrating a high degree of concurrence with offenders above, 11 supervisors stated that there is currently an over-reliance on menial tasks within the YOT and

DOI: 10.1057/9781137400468.0008

this is preventing the acquisition of employability skills. For example, two supervisors argued:

> *It all depends on the work placements available. Most of the time we are clearing rubbish or litter picking and there are no skills involved. It's just not skills orientated. The best placements I have supervised have been ones involving concreting or fencing. They* [young offenders] *go away having learnt something.* (Community reparation supervisor)

> *No, the placements are too easy for that. Litter picking doesn't involve a great deal of thought. There is no reason why it shouldn't but we need to stop litter picking and driving back and forth to the tip.* (Community reparation supervisor)

Nine supervisors expressed frustration and disappointment at the dominance of menial activities for offenders. In fact, an interesting finding to emerge from the interviews was that half the supervisors ($n = 6$) considered leaving the YOT, due to the monotony of the tasks. This is best illustrated through the following three comments:

> *The majority of placements are so basic that they are merely marking time. It is extremely frustrating and I have considered leaving on a number of occasions.* (Community reparation supervisor)

> *I thought that we would be doing jobs where I could teach the offenders but I just hand out black dustbin bags; fill the trailer and do dump runs. I'm not going to keep this up, its soul destroying.* (Community reparation supervisor)

> *All we do is drive to the tip with rubbish. The kids don't get anything from it and neither do I. I won't carry on much longer.* (Community reparation supervisor)

Throughout the two-year observation period, there has been a high turnover of reparation supervisors, with seven having left during this time. These findings are therefore important for YOT management, as they strongly suggest that the menial nature of the placements *could* be discouraging long-term employment within the YOT. Perhaps most importantly, they also indicate that while community reparation is capable of providing offenders with employability skills, the development of which can encourage long-term behavioural change and desistance from crime (McIvor, 1991; Downes, 1993; Chapman and Hough, 1998; Rex *et al.*, 2003; Curran *et al.*, 2007), an overreliance on menial tasks is preventing the acquisition of work-related skills for the high proportion of young people on the disposal.

YOT staff ($n = 8$) put forward several reasons for the lack of skills-based placements and there was no variation in responses. It was argued that shrub clearance work is readily available; extremely easy to find and organise; and ultimately requiring little effort from management. Menial placements also need limited equipment and such tasks carry little risk of breaching health and safety regulations or depriving others of paid employment (see YJB, 2011).

Perhaps most importantly, menial placements are inexpensive. Figures provided by the YOT show an overall annual budget for the reparation team of £150,000, divided between two sub-areas. Following deductions, including staff salaries; pension contributions; National Insurance and travel expenses, an approximate sum of £6000 remains, to cover the purchase of new cars, skips, tools, materials and health and safety equipment. Thus, there are virtually no funds available for innovative work schemes or the training of supervisors. Nonetheless, all 12 supervisors argued that more could be done to facilitate skills learning and they called for a more creative 'problem solving' approach. Crucially, this is a key element of CS provision that previous research shows is associated with rehabilitation and lower re-offending (Varah, 1981; McIvor, 1991, 1992; Holdaway *et al.*, 2001; Rex *et al.*, 2003; Wilcox and Hoyle, 2004; Curran *et al.*, 2007).

Problem solving

Young offenders were therefore asked to indicate whether their '*community reparation involved any problem solving*', the purpose of which was to explore the level of mental stimulation and challenge offered by placements (Varah, 1981; McIvor, 1991, 1992; Holdaway *et al.*, 2001; Rex *et al.*, 2003; Wilcox and Hoyle, 2004; Curran *et al.*, 2007). Again, the data reveals a statistically significant difference in mean scores between placement types. Offenders given menial activities were significantly *less likely* to indicate that any problem solving had occurred, producing a highly negative **mean** score of 1.9. In comparison, respondents given skills-based tasks gave a significantly higher positive **mean** score of 5.9 t $(95) = -8.82, p. <.0001$.

Due to the high proportion of offenders given menial placements, 62 respondents (64.6%) on such tasks, stated that their activities did not involve any form of problem solving. Similarly to the skills statement above, participants were extremely dissatisfied at the

DOI: 10.1057/9781137400468.0008

unchallenging nature of the work. This was summarised by three offenders as follows:

> *Clearing up other people's rubbish is not exactly hard. It's boring and stupid.* (Young person/Female)
>
> *No way does it involve any problem solving; breaking up wood is piss easy and a waste of time.* (Young person/Male)
>
> *The only problem solving is how quick I can get the litter in the shitty dustbin bag. What a joke.* (Young person/Male)

In contrast, those young people who completed skilled placements discussed a variety of positive and unexpected problem solving processes. In particular, 11 offenders (11.5%) suggested that the challenge and discipline of community reparation had prepared them for future employment. As two participants explained:

> *This has been hard work but it has been good for me. It has solved a problem for the future, coz I know that I want to be a painter and decorator.* (Young person/Male)
>
> *I'm knackered but this has really stepped me up to getting a job. Before this, I never knew what I wanted to do. Fencing is where it's at.* (Young person/Male)

Additionally, as table 4.3 shows, offenders (n = 10; 10.4%) given skilled placements also argued that their tasks had involved problem solving through processes of measurement or design, specifically relating to the building of bird boxes. Moreover, five offenders stated that they overcame difficulty regarding the felling of large trees, in order to replace damaged fencing. According to five participants, this entailed prior planning and teamwork.

YOT staff responded to whether *'community reparation involves problem solving'*, with a **mean** score of 5. Despite this positive level of agreement,

TABLE 4.3   *Offenders' qualitative responses to 'problem solving'*

Problem solving activity	Number of participants	% of sample
No problem solving activity involved in placement	62	64.6
Employment preparation	11	11.5
Measurement/Design	10	10.4
Tree felling	5	5.2
Planning and teamwork	5	5.2
N	93	

DOI: 10.1057/9781137400468.0008

all members of staff (n = 12) argued that the work is usually too menial to involve any 'direct' form of problem solving. As two supervisors explained:

> *The work isn't challenging enough. Offenders don't need to problem solve or even think for that matter.* (Community reparation supervisor)

> *Any problem solving would be accidental as the work is pretty easy for them to do.* (Community reparation supervisor)

Instead, ten supervisors believed that a level of long-term problem solving occurs within the supervisory process itself, through meaningful interaction between YOT worker and offender. Certainly, these findings suggest that staffs are encouraging a constructive working relationship and adopting a pro-social modelling approach within their supervision (Trotter, 1999). This is an important element of CS provision associated with rehabilitation (see McIvor, 1991, 1992, 2002; Gelsthorpe and Rex, 2004; Curran *et al.*, 2007). As three supervisors explained:

> *When you are working with these offenders, they talk to you openly about their problems and what has gone wrong in the past. They often seek a lot of advice and look to me. It actually seems to have a positive impact upon them. One once said to me, 'does everyone have problems at 15, or is it just me?' I was able to explain that he was not alone but it is the way we deal with these problems that is most important.* (Community reparation supervisor)

> *This work provides an opportunity for them to talk to someone in a non-judgemental setting. We discuss many issues and problems relating to their personal lives. I get them reflecting on the past and motivated for the future. They quickly learn that authority is not necessarily the enemy.* (Community reparation supervisor)

> *I do a lot of mentoring when working with these young people and they really talk openly and honestly and so we often discuss problems. CS is far better than talking to the young people in an office and across the desk, it is far more informal.* (Community reparation supervisor)

Due to this offender/staff interaction, supervisors (n = 7) also argued that community reparation is a useful engagement tool, in order to learn more about offenders and discover any underlying problems that may be contributing to their criminality. For instance, three members of staff stated:

> *Sometimes when we work one-on-one with a young person, they really open up and talk about their problems and ask for advice. Offenders have told me things that their case workers don't even know such as incidents of abuse. Reparation can be*

powerful at gaining intelligence and building rapport and it is far better than being in an office situation. (Community reparation supervisor)

When working with them [young people], you really get to know them well and all the troubles that they are having in their lives. It is sad but all this gets written up for the case workers and they are sometimes surprised by the level of detail that we have. (Community reparation supervisor)

If I had 5 hours working with a kid, I would know far more than a caseworker who works with someone for 5 months. (Community reparation supervisor)

Given the negative results profiled further above, especially in relation to a lack of skills provision, it can be argued that these staff views are partial and overly focused on the positive. Nevertheless, this is an encouraging finding to emerge as pro-social modelling (see Trotter, 1993; 1999) can lead to increased engagement; self-esteem; motivation; self worth; enhanced empathy or understanding and ultimately, positive behavioural change (Gelsthorpe and Rex, 2004; McIvor, 2002; Advisory Council on the Penal System, 1970).

In general, however, these research findings are negative. Whilst the results show that the disposal *can* be challenging and stimulating, for the majority of offenders given menial tasks, community reparation is neither interesting nor difficult. This represents a poor result for the YOT as previous research reviewed in Chapter 3 has shown the importance of engaging placements which motivate the offender (Varah, 1981; McIvor, 1991, 1992; Holdaway *et al.*, 2001; Rex *et al.*, 2003; Curran *et al.*, 2007). Indeed, offenders must perceive the process to be worthwhile and not a wholly punitive experience (Wilcox and Hoyle, 2004; Gray *et al.*, 2005).

Punishment

In order to further explore whether the disposal is perceived as a personally constructive or entirely negative experience, young offenders were asked to indicate if: '*community reparation is punishment*'. Demonstrating a relatively high level of agreement with this statement, offenders given menial tasks produced a **mean** score of 5.3. Crucially however, the skills-based sample provided a significantly better **mean** score of 2.8 t (95) = 4.82, $p <$ .0001, demonstrating that they did not see community reparation as an overly punitive response.

Differences in qualitative findings between the two groups are marked. Of those 74 offenders who completed the relatively unskilled tasks of shrub clearance, litter picking or 'kindling preparation', 58 participants (59.8%) argued strongly that the primary purpose of community reparation was punishment, in order to deter further offending. During assisted questionnaire completion, these respondents described the disposal in wholly negative terms, deriving no personal benefit from the experience. This is best illustrated through the following three comments:

> *It's punishment to make us think twice about offending again.* (Young offender/ Male)

> *Yeah its punishment. I hated every minute of it. That's what it's all about, to teach us a lesson.* (Young offender/Male)

> *Anything that they make you do that is painful is always going to be punishment.* (Young offender/Male)

The following statement typified the general feeling of these offenders:

> *Clearing up other peoples shit is punishment. How is it meant to help?* (Young offender/Male)

In comparison, the 23 offenders given skilled placements responded more positively, recognising some personal benefit to the work undertaken. In particular, young people ($n = 19$) argued that it was a constructive experience as the process had enabled them to gain new skills. For example, two offenders stated:

> *It's taught me a lot as well because I did not know how to make bird boxes.* (Young person/Male)

> *It's not like building a brick wall and kicking it down again.* [Supervisor's name] *taught me how to put down bricks. We are doing something worthwhile.* (Young person/Male)

YOT staff also indicated their level of agreement to an equivalent statement regarding punishment, producing a **mean** score of 5.8. A key finding to emerge from the interviews was that ten supervisors argued that, due to the menial nature of the work, community reparation will always be viewed as a punishment:

> *We make them clear other people's rubbish and they don't gain anything positive or helpful from doing so. Often the work is dirty and tedious, so to them, it's definitely a punishment.* (Community reparation supervisor)

> *Offenders hate the jobs that we do – its punishment pure and simple. It's a shame because they can gain a lot from the more involved jobs.* (Community reparation supervisor)

DOI: 10.1057/9781137400468.0008

It is hard to consider it anything other than a punishment, because of what we do. I don't think offenders are under any illusion that it isn't a punishment, the jobs ensure that! (Community reparation supervisor)

These research findings chime with the results above relating to skills acquisition and problem solving. They indicate that community reparation *can* be considered a useful disposal by offenders. However, due to the dominance of menial tasks, the majority of young people perceive the work to be a wholly negative and punitive experience. This is a discouraging result, as the research reviewed in Chapter 3 suggests that those who consider the work to be constructive or worthwhile are more receptive to positive behavioural change and desistance from crime (Wilcox and Hoyle, 2004; Gray *et al.*, 2005). This is especially true if offenders view the tasks as beneficial to the community (McIvor, 1991, 1992; Rex, 2001; Gray, 2005; Gray *et al.*, 2005; Curran *et al.*, 2007).

Benefits for the community

For this topic, the assisted questionnaire asked young offenders if the work undertaken on community reparation was '*good for the community*'. All 97 participants provided a highly positive overall **mean** score 6.5 (i.e. close to the maximum score of 7, *strongly agree* on the Likert scale) and there was no discernable difference between placement types. An examination of qualitative data reveals that 96 participants (98.9%) believed that their tasks had benefited the community in some way. In particular, 56 respondents (57.7%) stated that their community reparation had 'helped others', as shown through the following comment:

It helps people that cannot do it themselves. (Young person/Male)

Additionally, 40 offenders (41.2%) argued that their work had improved the appearance of the local area, primarily through rubbish clearance. This is best summarised by the young people themselves:

Everything around here was a shit hole before we came to clear it up. (Young person/Male)

I've cleared loads of rubbish and made the place look nicer for the community. (Young person/Female)

DOI: 10.1057/9781137400468.0008

All 12 YOT staff also believed that the work undertaken by offenders benefits the community, providing an identical and highly positive **mean** score of **6.5**. Typical comments made by supervisors are cited below:

> *Litter picking benefits us all.* (Community reparation supervisor)

> *We are doing what no one else wants to do and it is free labour, so it's good for the community.* (Community reparation supervisor)

> *Yes, it is good because this work would probably not be done otherwise.* (Community reparation supervisor)

Crucially however, ten supervisors qualified their responses by arguing that there was rarely an 'identifiable beneficiary', as the work is often undertaken in isolated locations and away from populations. For instance, two members of staff described their dissatisfaction as follows:

> *The work we do is generally good for the community because we clear up rubbish. However, it could be a lot better. Often we are doing work on a remote bit of scrubland and we don't actually know who we are working for. We could do a lot more for the elderly; vulnerable groups or those that are less fortunate.* (Community reparation supervisor)

> *The jobs are good for the community but it is not as good as it could be. We often work in random places that are out of the way, like wooded areas or parks. It would be good if the kids actually worked for someone.* (Community reparation supervisor)

This finding is supported by the observational and supervisory process. Certainly, over a two-and-a-half-year period, only one community reparation placement involved direct offender contact with an identifiable beneficiary. It is interesting to note that the young people on this particular task appeared far more engaged and motivated. In fact, both offenders asked to return to the project following completion of their reparation hours. This can be evidenced by the following comment:

> *When I was working on that disabled ramp, the lady looked really pleased and that gave me a good feeling. I was well pleased. She even gave me a cup of tea. Just hope we did a good job for her.* (Young person/Male)

Overall, these findings indicate that young offenders and staff perceive their work to be useful and worthwhile for the community, representing a positive result for the YOT (see also McIvor, 1991, 1992; Curran *et al.*, 2007). However, budgetary restrictions and the requirement not to undermine paid workers, means that limited placement options are available. Whilst menial or punitive tasks should not be cut completely, they need to be balanced against the development of elements of community reparation encouraging longer-term positive behavioural change (i.e. the acquisition of employability skills) (McGuire, 1995; Farrall, 2002; Hollin and Palmer, 2006). Moreover, this needs to be better publicised in order to improve the public's perception and to ensure that community reparation is seen as no 'soft option' (McIvor, 1991, 1992; Rex and Gelsthorpe, 2002; McCulloch, 2010).

The results above also demonstrate that direct offender contact with recipients is extremely rare. This is a dispiriting finding for the YOT, as research shows that reintegration (and thus desistance from crime) is more likely to occur if offenders are placed in positions which maximise contact with beneficiaries, requiring a level of reciprocity and exchange (McIvor, 1992, 2002; Gray *et al.*, 2005). Offenders are also more likely to believe that they have made amends, through direct reparation (Holdaway *et al.*, 2001; Wilcox and Hoyle, 2004; Gray *et al.*, 2005).

Reparation

Offenders were asked if the work undertaken during community reparation had '*made up for past offences*'. The purpose of this statement was to examine the perceived level of reparation offered by the disposal. The 74 young people given unskilled placements provided a weakly positive **mean** score of 4.8. Conversely, offenders that undertook skills-based tasks were more likely to indicate that a process of reparation had occurred, producing a significantly more positive **mean** score of 5.8 t (55.55) = -2.500, $p. < .015$.

Crucially, qualitative findings highlight an important link between the level of effort required to complete a task and offenders' perceptions of reparation. Twenty-one of the 74 young people that had undertaken shrub clearance, litter picking or 'kindling preparation' argued that the work was undemanding, requiring insufficient effort. Interestingly, these offenders appeared disappointed that they were unable to fully make amends for their offending. This is encapsulated in the three comments cited below:

> *Cutting a few branches wasn't difficult; it was easy and it hasn't made up for what I done.* (Young offender/Male)

> *How has this made up for it? Breaking up little pieces of wood for a couple of hours is a joke.* (Young offender/Male)

DOI: 10.1057/9781137400468.0008

> *I've been sat in the car for hours driving to the tip, no way has it put it right. It's shit.* (Young offender/Female)

On the other hand, 19 of the 23 young people who had completed skilled activities stated that they had worked hard in providing reparation, due to the testing nature of the tasks. It is important to note here, that challenge was not only associated with physical exertion, but also mental stimulation and thought. As two offenders stated:

> *I put loads into today* [fencing/ primary school] *and I'm knackered. I reckon I have made up for it.* (Young offender/Male)

> *It was really hard painting that room and I made it look good. I'm also covered. So yeah, I think I have put it right. I just want to move on.* (Young offender/Male)

Supervisory staff were also asked to indicate whether '*community reparation made up for past offences*', and in contrast to young offenders they produced a weakly negative **mean** score of 3.1, demonstrating disagreement with this statement. This topic prompted frank discussion but there was no variation in supervisors' qualitative remarks. All 12 supervisors believed that the work undertaken on community reparation was too easy, thus providing an inadequate level of reparation. As two supervisors explained:

> *I would have to think about this from the victim's point of view and I have to say that I would be irate if I knew the offender was required to sit in the car most of the day or do something as easy as litter picking. If I'm quite honest, that's what I would feel. It's equally frustrating for the kids that genuinely want to make things better.* (Community reparation supervisor)

> *Do you want an honest answer? Offenders want to make amends but I don't think the work we make them do is difficult. Most of the time they are chopping down bushes or driving to the dump and there is very little effort involved.* (Community reparation supervisor)

These research findings are highly significant as they show a connection between the challenge of a placement and a perception of adequate reparation. However, due to an over-reliance on menial tasks within the YOT, offenders and staff are frustrated at the simplistic and undemanding nature of the work, which is preventing young people from fully making amends. This is a similar picture to previous research studies into YJCR, reviewed in Chapter 3 (Holdaway *et al.*, 2001; Wilcox and Hoyle, 2004; Gray *et al.*, 2005). Perhaps most importantly, such an approach does not contribute to reductions in re-offending (see McIvor, 1992, 2002).

Attitudes toward re-offending

Towards the end of the assisted questionnaire, young offenders were asked to indicate whether: '*community reparation would stop them from re-offending in the future*'. Offenders given unskilled placements provided a weakly positive **mean** score of **4.9**, whereas participants that undertook skills-based activities produced a significantly higher positive **mean** score of **6.6** (i.e. extremely close to the highest possible mean score of 7, *strongly agree* on the Likert scale) $t (89.81) = -4.93, p < .0001$).

It is important to note here that respondents appeared reluctant to discuss their prospects regarding re-offending in any depth, thus qualitative data on this is limited. This could be due to the researcher's conflicting role of YJCR supervisor, perceived as an authoritative figure by the young people (see Bettencourt and Brown, 2003; McCoy, 1998 cited by Wilson, 2006, p.186). Nevertheless, of the 74 offenders given menial tasks, 39 participants stated that their decision to stop offending was based on the threat of imprisonment, rather than their experience of community reparation (see also Ellis, Pamment and Lewis, 2009, p. 405). This is illustrated through the following four comments:

> It's a warning before you get given the big stuff. If you get CS you'll just get prison next time. It's not worth it. (Young person/Female)

> I realise that this is my last chance to sort myself out. I don't want to go to prison. (Young person/Male)

> This has really made me buck up my ideas coz I realise that I am close to prison if I keep offending. (Young person/Male)

> It will stop me looking for trouble coz I know I'll get prison next time. (Young person/Male)

Importantly, 18 of the 23 offenders that had completed skilled activities stated that their confidence to stop offending originated from the work undertaken on community reparation. In particular, they suggested that the tasks had encouraged a greater consideration of the future, including employment opportunities. As three offenders stated:

> This has made me think about the future and it makes you not want to get in trouble anymore. I know I need a job, nothing special just something like this, you know working on a building site. (Young offender/Male)

> This has made me think about what I want to do with my life, I know I won't offend again coz I want a decent job. (Young offender/Male)

DOI: 10.1057/9781137400468.0008

Doing all this work you realise that you've been really stupid. Gives you loads of time to think about everything, like the future and that and jobs and stuff. (Young offender/Male)

YOT staff responded to an identical statement relating to whether 'community reparation stops offending in the future', producing a negative **mean** score of 3, in contrast to non-skills (4.9) and skills-based (6.6) offender groups. There was little variation in supervisors' qualitative responses and 11 members of staff argued that the disposal could not reduce re-offending in its current form. Supporting much of the earlier evidence reviewed in Chapter 3, supervisors argued that the majority of offenders do not gain anything from the process that would encourage long-term desistance from crime, such as employability skills (Rutter, Giller and Hagell, 1998; McGuire, 1995; Farrall, 2002; Hollin and Palmer, 2006). As three supervisors explained:

If we gave something positive to offenders for them to take away, like a basic skills certificate in painting or decorating, then they could gain employment which would prevent re-offending in the future. Simple clearance work is not actually giving them what they need. (Community reparation supervisor)

Community reparation has massive potential to stop offending but only if it is run properly. These guys need practical training and skills for a job. Until then, no, it won't stop offending. (Community reparation supervisor)

Not at the moment. Until we give offenders something positive to take away, this will always be known as the 'arse end' of the criminal justice system. (Community reparation supervisor)

Overall, these findings are significant as they show that offenders given skills-based placements are more likely to indicate that they will stop offending in the future, when compared to those given menial jobs (see also McIvor, 1992, p.153; Rex *et al.*, 2003, p. 63). Limited qualitative data suggests that such tasks may encourage offenders to reflect on the future and any employment opportunities. Crucially, supervisors also argued that menial tasks do not provide 'employability skills', which are crucial to reductions in re-offending (Lipsey, 1995; see also Farrington, 1996; 1997; McGuire, 1995; Farrall, 2002; Hollin and Palmer, 2006). It is important to note here, that YOT staff demonstrated an awareness of the factors identified within the earlier evaluation evidence, but arrived at through supervisory experience.

The purpose of this chapter was to present the main findings, which came out of the combined research methods used: secondary YOT case

DOI: 10.1057/9781137400468.0008

file data; participant observation; assisted questionnaires with young offenders and semi-structured interviews with supervisory staff. The following chapter draws together the themes from the preceding chapters and will bring to a conclusion the projects research findings.

Note

1   In order to interpret the results below, it is important to remember that the seven-point Likert scale is formulated so that a mean score of 1 represents absolute *disagreement* with a statement, and a mean score of 7 represents absolute *agreement* (see Miller, 1956; Gay, 1996; Robson, 2002).

DOI: 10.1057/9781137400468.0008

5

Conclusion: The Future Direction of Youth Justice Community Reparation

Abstract: *This chapter discusses the main conclusions that can be drawn from the research. It begins with a discussion of the key themes and findings from the earlier chapters, presenting established principles for the successful delivery of unpaid work for offenders. The chapter then goes on to assess the extent to which Youth Justice Community Reparation delivery in practice matches the evidence base. Finally, based on the key findings, it highlights major implications for future practice and identifies important areas for further research.*

Pamment, Nicholas. *Community Reparation for Young Offenders: Perceptions, Policy and Practice.* Basingstoke: Palgrave Macmillan, 2016. DOI: 10.1057/9781137400468.0009.

Discussion: key themes and findings

A major finding to emerge from this study is that little attention has been paid to the rehabilitative and re-integrative potential of unpaid work for offenders (Rex and Gelsthorpe, 2002; McCulloch, 2010). When adult community service was introduced in the early 1970s, the Advisory Council on the Penal System predicted that unemployed offenders would gain skills and a work ethic, combating social isolation and contributing to positive behavioural change (Advisory Council on the Penal System, 1970, par 34; Bergman, 1975; Duguid, 1982; Hine and Thomas, 1996; Rex and Gelsthorpe, 2002). However, throughout the 1980s, retributivsm dominated the political and policy agenda and there was a re-conceptualisation of community sentences, focusing on their ability to deliver 'tough' punishment (Hudson, 2003; Garland, 2001; Muncie, 1999; Faulkner and Burnett, 2011). What followed was 30 years of consecutive legislative changes, emphasising the punitive power of adult community service, culminating in the politically inspired *Community Payback* initiative in 2008 (Worrall, 1997; Carter, 2003; Casey, 2008).

Crucially, therefore, YJCR was introduced in the Crime and Disorder Act (CDA) 1998, at a time when retribution was already the main focus established for adult community service (Rex and Gelsthorpe, 2002; Maruna and King, 2008; Wasik, 2008; Faulkner and Burnett, 2011). Consequently, the reparative aspect of the work quickly became synonymous with punishment (Haines and O'Mahony, 2006; Stephenson, Giller and Brown, 2007). Indeed, Holdaway *et al.* (2001, p. 37) claimed that community reparation was the least effective disposal for preventing recidivism and its rehabilitive potential was ignored.

This study has argued that it was wrong to dismiss YJCR in this way as it has the potential to be a highly successful re-integrative intervention for young people. By integrating the evidence-base for both adult CS and YJCR, drawn together within Chapter 3, this research shows more consistently that unpaid work can have a positive impact on offenders in a number of ways.

Through the completion of unpaid work, offenders can gain skills suitable for employment (Varah, 1981; McIvor, 1991, 1992; Rex *et al.*, 2003), a well-established key factor associated with reductions in re-offending (Rutter, Giller and Hagell, 1998; McGuire, 1995; Farrall, 2002; Hollin and Palmer, 2006). Placements can also motivate offenders, facilitating positive behavioural change and the work itself can provide the opportunity

DOI: 10.1057/9781137400468.0009

to fully 'make amends' (Rex *et al.*, 2003; Curran *et al.*, 2007; McIvor, 1991, 1992; Wilcox and Hoyle, 2004).

Whilst there is evidence that unpaid work is capable of reducing recidivism for both adult and young offenders (Lloyd *et al.*, 1994; May, 1999; Jennings, 2003; Spicer and Glicksman, 2004; Ministry of Justice, 2011b), this research has shown that there are important detailed qualifications relating to the delivery and organisation of the disposal, which, if not in place, will reduce the chances of successful outcomes. Certainly, as summarised in Figure 5.1, the evidence base shows that offenders must be provided with a variety of 'meaningful' work placements, which are not perceived as menial, repetitive or boring by offenders and/or supervisors (Varah, 1981; McIvor, 1992; Holdaway *et al.*, 2001; Wilson and Wahidin, 2006). To be successful, unpaid work placements must also facilitate the

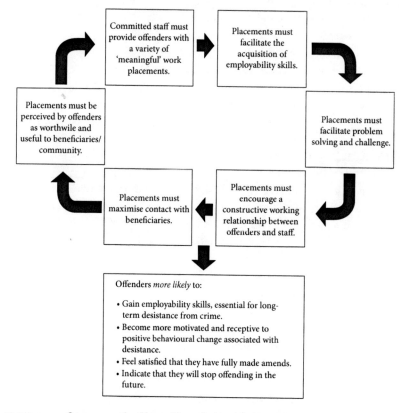

FIGURE 5.1   *Summary of evidenced-based principles for the delivery of unpaid work most likely to lead to successful outcomes*

DOI: 10.1057/9781137400468.0009

acquisition of employability skills and they should be engaging, involving a level of problem solving and stimulation (Wilcox and Hoyle, 2004; Curran *et al.*, 2007). The work should also maximise contact with beneficiaries, ensuring that the process is perceived by offenders as worthwhile and helpful to the community (McIvor, 1991, 1992; Gray, 2005).

It is suggested that Figure 5.1 could be utilised to develop an evidenced-based best practice model for YJCR. In particular, it could be used by HM Inspectorate of Probation (HMIP) to develop more effective inspection criteria (Ministry of Justice, 2012c). This would be a significant development, as currently no information exists relating to the successful delivery of YJCR. Instead, guidance provided by the YJB on how to develop and improve YJCR, as part of the Youth Crime Action Plan, makes no mention of the key elements of delivery which are most likely to lead to successful outcomes (see YJB, 2008). The reasons for this seem clear. Firstly, there is a lack of priority afforded to the re-integrative potential of YJCR. Secondly, there is a lack of high quality evaluation on the disposal, resulting in ignorance of its re-integrative potential (Hazel, Hagell and Brazier, 2002; Rex and Gelsthorpe, 2002). It is, therefore, unsurprising that the results from the primary research into YJCR in practice are, on balance, negative.

Key conclusions: YJCR in practice

As noted, the key finding about YJCR delivery in practice is that it does not match the available evidence base of what is thought to be effective. Limited, but available, national studies assessed in Chapter 3, indicate that community reparation is not being operated effectively by YOTs (Holdaway *et al.*, 2001; Wilcox and Hoyle, 2004; Gray *et al.*, 2003; Gray *et al.*, 2005). Crucially, the first in-depth primary research undertaken within this study further supports these findings. It has uncovered serious inadequacies and failings regarding the organisation and delivery of the disposal, which severely limited any potential to reduce re-offending.

Rather than implementing the effective principles for the delivery of unpaid work summarised in Figure 5.1, the YOT 'case study' area has adopted a formulaic approach to workplace provision, providing a narrow range of low cost placements. There is, therefore, an over-reliance on menial tasks, with 76% of participants completing shrub clearance, litter picking or kindling preparation. As a result, both offenders and their supervisors were frustrated and disappointed that such placements did not facilitate the acquisition of employability skills. If this approach is repeated nationally (and finding this out should be an urgent consideration for the YJB), this could help explain the increasingly high reconviction rates for the reparation order as funding is decreased (Jennings, 2003; Whiting and Cuppleditch, 2006; Ministry of Justice, 2011a), while adult unpaid work continues to reduce re-offending (Spicer and Glicksman, 2004).

In this case study, the low skills content and menial nature of three quarters of YJCR work meant that the majority of offenders were unable to fully 'make amends' for their offending. Furthermore, they were not interested, stimulated or challenged by the placements, which rarely had any identifiable beneficiary. YOT staff also experienced disillusionment and nine of the 12 supervisors had considered leaving the YOT. One supervisor likened the activities to '*voluntary refuse collection*'. Thus, instead of being considered a 'worthwhile' or 'helpful' process, YJCR was perceived primarily as a punitive experience by all participants and to a large extent, even the staff (see also Holdaway *et al.*, 2001; Wilcox and Hoyle, 2004; Gray *et al.*, 2005).

If the intention is purely retributive, as the changes discussed above in legislation over a long period tend to indicate (see Faulkner and Burnett, 2011, pp. 127–128), this might be seen positively. However, punishment alone does not contribute to long-term desistance from crime (McSweeney *et al.*, 2006; Worrall, 1997) and the evidence base presented suggests that it would be more profitable to focus on worthwhile activities that can engage and motivate offenders and on facilitating direct contact with beneficiaries as a positive re-integrative process, encouraging lasting behavioural change (McIvor, 1992, 2002; Gray *et al.*, 2005, p. 945). There is an important coda here in that the purpose, content and impact of such placements need to be better publicised, in order to improve the public's perception and to ensure that YJCR is not seen as a 'soft option' (YJB, 2008). In short, the agenda might be shifted from a focus on being tough, to one of effectiveness in terms of lower reconvictions, and ultimately, cost-effectiveness, if there is political will to do so.

In this study, despite the poor delivery of YJCR and the clear disillusionment of staff, there was some evidence that supervisors were adopting a pro-social modelling approach (Trotter, 1993; 1999; HMIP, 1998; Raynor, 1998), with a clear employability focus. In particular, staff were working hard to act as positive role models, instilling a work ethic through support, guidance, motivation, reward and advice regarding pro-criminal attitudes (see also McIvor, 2002; Gelsthorpe and Rex, 2004; Curran *et al.*, 2007; McCulloch, 2010). Indeed, the observational work showed a striking mismatch between the relatively high level of commitment of the supervisors and the relatively weak organisation of the disposal. The words of a reparation supervisor typify the overall qualitative observational findings within this study:

> *I have worked with some really committed and enthusiastic supervisors who try and engage the young people at every opportunity. You must remember that most of them give up their time without any pay and they can bring a lifetime of skills and experience. They can only do so much when being directed from above and they would deliver good stuff if they were able to.* (Community reparation supervisor)

This imbalance between the aspirations of the supervisors and the limited capability of the available placements to match them resulted in only a minority of offenders being given skills-based placements and these were significantly *more likely* to: gain employability skills; be meaningfully engaged and motivated within the supervisory process; feel satisfied that they have fully made amends and most importantly, indicate that they will stop offending in the future (see also McIvor, 1992; Rex *et al.*, 2003; Curran *et al.*, 2007).

Offenders and supervisors made several suggestions for changes to community reparation. The staff advocated a 'root and branch' reform of the disposal. Most importantly, and in line with the general argument of this book, participants called for a greater variety of placements, in order to avoid menial tasks and gain employability skills. YOT staff argued that management could adopt a more 'imaginative' approach to workplace provision, necessitating the allocation of further funds to facilitate skills orientated placements and ongoing supervisor training and development. It seems that experientially, both young offenders and supervisors have come to the same conclusions as the evaluation evidence. All it needs now is for legislators and policy makers to listen and act upon it. A number of implications for practice logically flow from the suggestions above and the overall findings of this research.

Implications for practice

Firstly, more attention needs to be paid to the rehabilitative potential of YJCR. Consecutive governments have called for more 'robust' unpaid work. This current political focus could be positively exploited if further

DOI: 10.1057/9781137400468.0009

resources are provided in the coming years, to enable the development and promotion of positive and *effective* elements of the disposal, influencing long-term desistance from crime, especially the acquisition of employability skills.

Secondly, YOTs should provide offenders (and staff) with a variety of meaningful work placements. These should facilitate the acquisition of employability skills and involve a level of problem solving and challenge. Placements should also maximise offender contact with beneficiaries. If these elements are in place, they will also maximise the potential for offenders to perceive their placements as worthwhile and useful. These established principles of evidence that maximise the likelihood of reductions in re-offending and wider rehabilitative effects of YJCR, should be disseminated to YOTs in the form of an 'evidenced-based best practice model'. After which, YJCR could be assessed against these criteria by HM Inspectorate of Probation, which will contribute to increasing staff awareness and commitment to the disposal.

Thirdly, an evidenced-based best practice model should also be disseminated to sentencers. Indeed, the courts need a greater level of understanding of YJCR and its re-integrative potential. This could positively affect sentencing behaviour, diverting young offenders away from the damaging environment of custody (Carlile Inquiry, 2006; Faze, Benning and Danesh, 2005; Goldson, 2006) and other ineffective disposals, such as Intensive Supervision and Surveillance (ISS) (Ellis, Pamment and Lewis, 2009; Howard League for Penal Reform, 2011). Emphasising the effectiveness of YJCR would enable sentencing and the allocation of YOT budgets to be harmonised (see also Sutton, 2010), but it will also empower sentencers to demand YJCR orders that have evidence-based content and delivery.

Placements adhering to the above principles need to be better publicised, in order to improve the public's perception and to ensure that YJCR is not seen as an easy option. This could be achieved through the utilisation of local media or local information newsletters, showcasing stories and case examples of best practice, thus improving local community knowledge and confidence. Additionally, plaques should be used to show where work has been completed by offenders and these could be sponsored by local businesses (see also Carter, 2003; Casey, 2008; YJB, 2008).

Finally, there should be a specific budget allocation for the provision of skills-based placements, equipment and the ongoing training and development of YJCR supervisors. This money should be 'ring fenced' and not consumed within the general administration of the disposal.

DOI: 10.1057/9781137400468.0009

This might be more possible within the existing overall budget allocation to YOTs, as increased sentencer confidence in community reparation would enable resources to be redirected from poorly performing disposals, such as ISS.

Limitations and implications for future research

Whilst this study has significantly added to the knowledge base regarding unpaid work in general and YJCR in particular, it has some obvious limitations. Due to the inevitable resource constraints, the sample obtained within this research may not be representative of the national picture. Moreover, whilst it has provided a contemporary snapshot of offenders on YJCR, this study was unable to examine more detailed secondary data and take into consideration past offenders that have been subject to community reparation.

Given these limitations, there are key areas for future research. Most importantly, there is an urgent need for a national study, of a similar design, which incorporates both adult CS and YJCR. Specifically, whilst it was beyond the scope of this study, further research is required into probation run unpaid work placements for 16 and 17 year olds (Sutton, 2010). Indeed, the YOTs' delivery of community reparation is substantively different from the probation services' delivery of unpaid work for young offenders. Therefore, further research is needed to examine the relationship between financial resources, evidence-based best practice, reconviction performance, and delivery by YOTs or probation services, including outsourced provision.

Best practice may, to some extent, be a function of available financial resources (Sutton, 2010). Thus, beyond this study, a comprehensive national cost-benefit analysis should be carried out comparing probation service and YOT delivery of YCJR, to establish whether: there is a preferable mode of delivery in relation to reductions in re-offending; and the appropriate threshold/unit cost of unpaid work placements in order to deliver evidence-based content. In this time of extreme austerity, this could make a valuable contribution to contemporary policy and practice, through possible reductions in the use of imprisonment and its associated costs, while ensuring that 'robust' evidence-based community penalties are delivered to reduce re-offending.

DOI: 10.1057/9781137400468.0009

Bibliography

Advisory Council on the Penal System. (1970). *Non-Custodial and Semi-Custodial Penalties*. London: HMSO.

Aebi, M., Delgrande, N. and Marguet, Y. (2009). *Non-Custodial Sanctions and Measures Served in 2009*. Retrieved from: http://www3.unil.ch/wpmu/space/files/2011/02/Council-of-Europe_SPACE-II-2009-E.pdf.

Allen, G. F. and Treger, H. (1990). Community Service Orders in Federal Probation: Perceptions of Probationers and Host Agencies. *Federal Probation*, 54(3), pp. 8–23.

Andrews, D. (1995). The Psychology of Criminal Conduct and Effective Treatment. In J. McGuire (Ed.), *What Works: Reducing Re-offending: Guidelines from Research and Practice* (pp. 35–62). Chichester, UK: Wiley.

Andrews D. A., Keissling J. J., Russell R. J. and Grant B. A. (1979). *Volunteers and the One to One Supervision of Adult Probationers*. Toronto: Ministry of Correctional Services.

Audit Commission. (1996). *Misspent Youth: Young People and Crime*. London: Audit Commission.

Bain, A. and Parkinson, G. (2010). Resettlement and Social Rehabilitation: Are We Supporting Success? *Probation Journal*, 57(1), pp. 63–74.

Baker, K. (2004). Is *Asset* Really an Asset? Risk Assessment of Young Offenders. In Burnett, R. and Roberts, C. (Eds), *What Works in Probation and Youth Justice: Developing Evidence-Based Practice* (pp. 46–70). Cullompton, Willan.

Baker, K., Jones, S., Roberts, C. and Merrington, S. (2002). Validity and Reliability of Asset: Findings from the First Two Years of the Use of Asset. London: YJB.

Barry, M. (2000). The Mentor / Monitor Debate in Criminal Justice: 'What Works' for Offenders, *British Journal of Social Work, 30*(5), pp. 575–595.

Barry, M., McNeil, F. and Lightowler, C. (2009). *Youth Offending and Youth Justice* (Briefing paper). Retrieved from: http://www.sccjr.ac.uk/pubs/Youth-Offending-and-Youth-Justice/162.

Bateman, T. and Pitts, J. (2005). 'Conclusion: What the Evidence Tells Us'. In T. Bateman and J. Pitts (Eds), *The RHP Companion to Youth Justice* (pp.248–258). Lyme Regis: Russell House Publishing.

Bergman, H. D. (1975). Community Service in England: An Alternative to Custodial Sentence. *Federal Probation, 39*, pp. 43–46.

Bettencourt, L. A. and Brown, S. W. (2003). Role Stressors and Customer-Oriented Boundary-Spanning Behaviours in Service Organizations. *Journal of the Academy of Marketing Science, 31* (4), pp. 394–408.

Bottomley, A. K. and Pease, K. (1993). *Crime and Punishment: Interpreting the data.* Milton Keynes: Open University Press.

Bottoms, A. (1995). The Politics of Sentencing Reform. In R. Morgan (Ed.), *The Philosophy and Politics of Punishment and Sentencing* (pp. 17–49). Oxford: Oxford University Press.

Bottoms, A. (2008). The Community Dimensions of Community Penalties. *The Howard Journal, 47*(2), pp. 146–169.

Bottoms, A. and Dignan, J. (2004). *Youth Crime and Youth Justice: Comparative and Cross-national Perspectives.* Chicago: University of Chicago Press.

Bottoms, A. E. (1987). Limiting Prison Use in England and Wales. *Howard Journal, 26*, pp. 177–202.

Brace, N., Kemp, R. and Snelgar, R. (2009). *SPSS for Psychologists* (4th Edition). London: Palgrave Macmillan.

Braithwaite, J. and Pettit, P. (1990). *Not Just Deserts: A Republican Theory of Criminal Justice.* Oxford: Oxford University Press.

Bryman, A. (2008). *Social Research Methods* (3rd edition). Oxford: Oxford University Press.

Burnett, R. and Appleton, C. (2004). Joined-up Services to Tackle Youth Crime. *British Journal of Criminology, 44*(1), pp. 34–54.

Burnett, R. and Roberts, C. (2004). *What Works in Probation and Youth Justice: Developing Evidence Based Practice.* Cullumpton: Willan.

DOI: 10.1057/9781137400468.0010

Campbell, B. (1993). *Goliath: Britain's Dangerous Places*. London: Methuen.

Carlile Inquiry. (2006). *An independent inquiry into the use of physical restraint, solitary confinement and forcible strip searching of children in prisons, secure training centres and local authority secure children's homes*. London: Howard League for Penal Reform.

Carter, C. (2007). *Offenders and Nature: Helping People – Helping Nature*. Farnham: Forest Research.

Carter, C. and Pycroft, A. (2010). Getting Out: Offenders in Forestry and Conservation Work Settings. In J. Brayford, F. Cowe and J. Deering (Eds), *What Else Works? Creative Work with offenders* (pp.211–236). Uffculme: Willan Publishing.

Carter, N., Klein, R. and Day, P. (1992). *How Organisations Measure Success – the Use of Performance Indicators in Government*. London: Routledge.

Carter, P. (2003). *Managing Offenders, Reducing Crime: A New Approach*. London: Home Office.

Cartledge, G. C. (1986). Community Service in England/Wales: Organization and Implementation of Community Service: An Evaluation and Assessment of Its Outcomes. In H. Albrecht and W. Schadler (Eds), *Community Service: A New Option in Punishing Offenders in Europe*. Freiburg: Max Planck Institute for Foreign and International Penal Law.

Casey, L. (2008). *Engaging Communities in Fighting Crime: A Review*. London: Cabinet Office.

Chapman, T. and Hough, M. (1998). *Evidence Based Practice: A Guide to Effective Practice*. London: HM Inspectorate of Probation.

CIPD. (2004). *Employing Ex-Offenders: A Practical Guide*. London: Chartered Institute of Personnel and Development.

Clark, D. A. (2000). *Theory Manual for Enhanced Thinking Skills. Prepared for the Joint Prison-Probation Accreditation Panel*. London: Home Office.

Clarke, K. (2011). *Kenneth Clarke Blames English Riots on a Broken Penal System*. Retrieved from: http://www.guardian.co.uk/uk/2011/sep/05/ kenneth-clarke-riots-penal-system.

Crawford, A. and Newburn, T. (2002). Recent Developments in Restorative Justice for Young People in England and Wales, *British Journal of Criminology*, 42(3), pp. 476–495.

Cunliffe, J. and Shepherd, A. (2007). *Re-Offending of Adults: Results from the 2004 Cohort, Home Office Statistical Bulletin 06/07*. London: Home Office.

DOI: 10.1057/9781137400468.0010

Curran, J., MacQueen, S., Whyte, B. and Boyle, J. (2007). *Forced to Make Amends: An Evaluation of the Community Reparation Orders Pilot* (Crime and Justice Research Findings No 95). Retrieved from: http://www.scotland.gov.uk/Resource/Doc/195674/0052459.pdf.

Delens-Ravier, I. (2003). Juvenile Offenders' Perceptions of Community Service. in L. Walgrave (Ed.), *Repositioning Restorative Justice* (pp. 149–166). Portland, OR: Willan.

Department of Health and Home Office. (1992). *Review of Health and Social Services for Mentally Disordered Offenders: Final Summary Report* (Reed Report) (Cm 2088). London: Stationery Office.

DeWalt, K. M. and DeWalt, B. R. (1998). Participant Observation. In H. R, Bernard (Ed.), *Handbook of Methods in Cultural Anthropology* (pp. 259–300). Walnut Creek: AltaMira Press.

Dignan, J. (2005). *Understanding Victims and Restorative Justice.* Maidenhead: Open University Press.

Downes, D. (1993). *Employment Opportunities for Offenders.* London: Home Office.

Dugmore, P., Pickford, J. and Angus, S. (2006). *Transforming Social Work Practice: Youth Justice and Social Work.* Exeter: Learning Matters.

Duguid, S. (1982). Rehabilitation through Education: A Canadian Model. *Journal of Offender Counselling, Services and Rehabilitation,* 6, pp. 53–68.

Easton, S. and Piper, C. (2005). *Sentencing and Punishment: The Quest for Justice.* Oxford: Oxford University Press.

Ellis, T. and Boden, I. (2005). *Is There a Unifying Professional Culture in Youth Offending Teams? A Research Note.* Retrieved from: http://www.britsoccrim.org/volume7/006.pdf.

Ellis, T., Hedderman, C. and Mortimer, E. (1996). *Enforcing Community Sentences: Supervisors' Perspectives on Ensuring Compliance and Dealing with Breach.* Home Office Research Study, 158, London: Home Office.

Ellis, T., Pamment, N. and Lewis, C. (2009). Public Protection in Youth Justice? The Intensive Supervision and Surveillance Programme (ISSP) from the Inside. *International Journal of Police Science and Management,* 11(4), pp. 393–413.

Ellis, T. and Savage, S. (2012). Restorative Justice or Retribution? In T. Ellis, T. and S. P Savage (Eds), *Debates in Criminal Justice: Key Themes and Issues* (pp. 78–116). Oxford: Routledge.

Ellis, T. and Underdown, A. (1998). *Evaluation and the Evidence Base. Strategies for Effective Offender Supervision. Report of the HMIP What Works project.* London: HMIP.

Ellis, T. and Winstone, J. (2002). The Policy Impact of a Survey of Programme Evaluations in England and Wales: Towards a New Corrections-Industrial Complex? In, J. McGuire (Ed.), *Offender Rehabilitation and Treatment: Effective Programmes and Policies to Reduce Re-offending* (pp. 333–359). Chichester: Wiley.

Farrall, S. (2002). *Rethinking What Works with Offenders: Probation, Social Context and Desistance from Crime.* Collumpton: Willan Publishing.

Farrall, S. (2004). Social Capital and Offender Re-integration: Making Probation Desistance Focused. In S. Maruna and R. Immarigeon (Eds), *After Crime and Punishment: Pathways to Offender Reintegration* (pp. 57–82). Cullompton, Devon: Willan.

Farrington, D. (1996). the Explanation and Prevention of Youthful Offending. In J. D. Hawkins (Ed.), *Delinquency and Crime* (pp. 257–282). U.S.A: Cambridge University Press.

Farrington, D. (1997). Early Prediction of Violent and Non-Violent Youthful Offending. *European Journal on Criminal Policy and Research,* 5(2), pp. 51–66.

Faulkner, D. and Burnett, R. (2011). *Where Next for Criminal Justice?* Bristol: Policy Press.

Faze, S., Benning, R. and Danesh, J. (2005). Suicides in Male Prisoners in England and Wales 1978–2003. *The Lancet, 366,* pp.1301–1302.

Francis, P. and Padel, U. (2000). Editorial: Youth Justice. *Criminal Justice Matters, 41,* p. 3.

Fricker, M. (2008). *Criminals Take Six Months to Paint Eight Railings during Their Community Service.* Retrieved from: http://www.mirror.co.uk/news/top-stories/2008/05/28/criminals-take-six-months-to-paint-eight-railings-during-their-community-service-115875-20432129/.

Garland, D. (2001). *The Culture of Control: Crime and social order in contemporary society* Oxford: Oxford University Press.

Garrett, C. G. (1985). Effects of Residential Treatment on Adjudicated Delinquents: A Meta-Analysis, *Journal of Research in Crime and Delinquency, 22,* pp. 287–308.

Gavrielides, T. (2008). Restorative Justice: The Perplexing Concept. Conceptual Fault Lines and Power Battles within the Restorative Justice Movement. *Criminology and Criminal Justice Journal, 8(2),* pp. 165–183.

Gay, L. (1996). *Educational Research: Competencies for Analysis and Application.* New Jersey: Prentice Hall.

DOI: 10.1057/9781137400468.0010

Gelsthorpe, L. and Rex, S. (2004). Community Service as Reintegration: Exploring the Potential. In: G. Mair (Ed.), *What Matters in Probation* (pp. 229–254). Cullompton: Willan.

Glass, G. V., McGaw, B. and Smith, M. L. (1981). *Meta-Analysis in Social Research*. Beverly Hills, CA: Sage.

Goldblatt, P. and Lewis, C. (Eds), (1998). *Reducing Offending: An Assessment of Research Evidence on Ways of Dealing with Offending Behaviour*. Home Office Research Study No. 187. London: Home Office.

Goldson, B. (2001). A Rational Youth Justice? Some Critical Reflections on the Research, Policy and Practice Relation. *Probation Journal*. 48(2), pp. 76–85.

Goldson, B. (2006). Damage, Harm and Death in Child Prisons: Questions of Abuse and Accountability. *The Howard Journal of Criminal Justice*, 45(5), pp. 449–467.

Gorman, K. (2001). Cognitive Behaviourism and the Holy Grail: The Quest for a Universal Means of Managing Offender Risk, *Probation Journal*, 48(1), pp. 3–9.

Gray, E., Roberts, C., Merrington, S., Waters, I., Fernandez, R. and Hayward, G. (2005). *ISSP: The Final Report*. London: Youth Justice Board.

Gray, P., Moseley, J. and Browning, R. (2003). *An Evaluation of the Plymouth Restorative Justice Programme*. Plymouth: University of Plymouth.

Gray, P. (2005). The Politics of Risk and Young Offenders' Experiences of Social Exclusion and Restorative Justice, *British Journal of Criminology*, 45(6), pp. 938–957.

Grubin D. and Thornton, D. (1994). A National Programme for the Assessment and Treatment of Sex Offenders in the English Prison System, *Criminal Justice and Behaviour*, 21, pp. 55–71.

Haines, K. and O'Mahony, D. (2006). Restorative Approaches: Young People and Youth Justice. In B, Goldson and R, Morgan (Eds), *Youth Crime and Justice* (pp. 110–124). London: Sage.

Harris, R. and Lo, W. (2002). Community Service: Its use in Criminal Justice. *International Journal of Offender Therapy and Comparative Criminology*, 46(4), pp. 427–444.

Hayden, C. and Gough, C. (2010). *Implementing Restorative Justice in Children's Residential Care*. Bristol: Policy Press.

DOI: 10.1057/9781137400468.0010

Hazel, N., Hagell, A. and Brazier, L. (2002). *Young People' Perceptions of Their Experiences of the Criminal Justice System.* End of award report to the ESRC.

Hedderman, C. and Sugg, D. (1997). *The Influence of Cognitive Approaches: A Survey of Probation Programmes, Changing Offenders' Attitudes and Behaviour: What Works?*, Home Office Research Study, no. 171, London: Home Office.

Her Majesty's Inspectorate of Prisons for England and Wales. (1997). *Young Prisoners: A Thematic Review by HM Chief Inspector of Prisons for England and Wales.* London: Home Office.

Hine, J. and Celnick, A. (2001). *A One Year Reconviction Study of Final Warnings* RDS 05/01. London: HMSO.

Hine, J. and Thomas, N. (1996). Evaluating Work with Offenders: Community Service Orders. In G. McIvor (Ed.), *Working with Offenders.* London: Jessica Kingsley.

HM Inspectorate of Probation (HMIP). (1998). *Strategies for Effective Offender Supervision: Report of the HMIP What Works Project.* Home Office: London.

Holdaway, S., Davidson, N., Dignan, J., Hammersley, R., Hine, J. and Marsh, P. (2001). *New Strategies to Address Youth Offending – the National Evaluation of the Pilot Youth Offending Teams.* RDS Occasional Paper No 69, London, Home Office.

Hollin, C. R. and Palmer, E. J. (Eds), (2006). *Offending Behaviour Programmes: Development, Application and Controversies.* Chichester: John Wiley & Sons.

Holt, A. and Pamment, N. (2011). Overcoming the Challenges of Researching 'Young Offenders': Using Assisted Questionnaires – a Research Note. *International Journal of Social Research Methodology, 14*(2), pp. 125–133.

Home Office. (1969). *People in Prison.* London: HMSO.

Home Office. (1983). *Probation Statistics England and Wales 1983.* London: HMSO.

Home Office. (1988). *Punishment, Custody and the Community.* Cm 424.

Home Office. (1990). *Crime Justice and Protecting the Public.* Cm. 965.

Home Office. (1992). *National Standards for the Supervision of Offenders in the Community.* London: Home Office.

Home Office. (1993). *Reconvictions of Those Given Probation and Community Service Orders in 1987 (Home Office Statistical Bulletin 18/93).* London: Home Office.

DOI: 10.1057/9781137400468.0010

Home Office. (1995a). *National Standards for the Supervision of Offenders in the Community*. London: Home Office.

Home Office. (1995b). *Criminal Statistics: England and Wales 1994*. Cm.3010. London: HMSO.

Home Office. (1995c). *Visible Unpaid Work (66/2005)*. London Home Office.

Home Office. (1997). *No More Excuses – A New Approach to Tackling Youth Crime in England and Wales*, Cm 3809. London: Home Office.

Home Office. (1998). *The Crime and Disorder Act: Reparation Orders*. Retrieved from http://www.nationalarchives.gov.uk/ERORecords/HO/421/2/cdact/repord.htm.

Home Office. (2004). *Reducing Re-offending National Action Plan*. London: Home Office.

Home Office. (2006). *A Five Year Strategy for Protecting the Public and Reducing Re-offending*, Cm 6717. London: The Stationery Office.

Hosmer, D.W., and Lemeshow, S. (2000). *Applied Logistic Regression*. New York: Wiley.

Hough, M. and Roberts, V. J. (2004). *Youth Crime and Youth Justice: Public Opinion in England and Wales*. Bristol: The Policy Press.

Howard League for Penal Reform. (2011). *Life Outside: Collective Identity, Collective Exclusion*. Retrieved from: http://www.howardleague.org/life-outside/.

Huang, C., Liao, H. and Chang, S. (1998). Social Desirability and the Clinical Self-Report Inventory: Methodological Reconsideration. *Journal of Clinical Psychology*, 54(4), pp. 517–528.

Hudson, B. (2003). *Understanding Justice: An Introduction to Ideas, Perspectives and Controversies in Modern Penal Theory*. Buckingham: Open University Press.

Hudson, J., and Galaway, B. (1990). Community service: Toward Program Definition. *Federal Probation*, 54, pp. 3–9.

Hunter, J. E. and Schmidt, F. L. (1990). *Methods of Meta-Analysis: Correcting Error and Bias in Research Findings*. Newbury Park, CA: Sage.

Jenks, C. (1996). *Childhood*. London: Routledge.

Jennings, D. (2003). *One Year Juvenile Reconviction Rates: First Quarter of 2001 Cohort*. Online Report 18/3. London: Home Office.

Johnson, P. and Ingram, B. (2007). Windows of Opportunity for Unpaid Work? *Probation Journal*, 54(1), pp. 62–69.

Johnson, T. and Fendrich, M. (2002). *A Validation of the Crowne-Marlowe Social Desirability Scale*. Retrieved from: http://www.srl.uic.edu/publist/Conference/crownemarlowe.pdf.

DOI: 10.1057/9781137400468.0010

Jones, D. (2002). Questioning New Labour's Youth Justice Strategy: A Review Article, *Youth. Justice*, *1*(3), pp. 14–26.

Jupp, V. (1989). *Methods of Criminological Research*. London: Unwin Hyman.

Jupp, V., Davies, P. and Francis, P. (Eds), (2000). *Doing Criminological Research*. London: Sage.

Kaye, R. and Gibbs, B. (2010). *Fitting the Crime. Reforming Community Sentences: Mending the Weak Link in the Sentencing Chain*. London: Policy Exchange.

Kershaw, C. (1999). *Reconvictions of Offenders Sentenced or Discharged from Prison in 1994. Home Office Statistical Bulletin*. London: Home Office.

Kerslake, B. (2011). *Restorative Justice in the Youth Justice System*. Retrieved from: www.remediuk.org/Bill%20Kerslake%20Remedi%20 YJB%20-.ppt.

Kemshall, H. (2002). Effective Practice in Probation: An Example of 'Advanced Liberalism Responsibilisation', *Howard Journal*, *41*(1), pp. 41–58.

Kendall, K. (2004). Dangerous Thinking: A Critical History of Correctional Cognitive Behaviourism. In G. Mair (Ed.), *What Matters in Probation* (pp. 53–89). Cullompton: Willan.

Killias, M., Aebi, M. and Ribeaud, D. (2000). Does Community Service Rehabilitate Better Than Short-Term Imprisonment? Results of a Controlled Experiment, *The Howard Journal*, *39*(1), pp. 40–57.

King, M. and Bruner, G. (2000). Social Desirability Bias: A Neglected Aspect of Validity Testing. *Psychology and Marketing*, *17*(2), pp.79–103.

Knapp, M., Robertson, E. and McIvor, G. (1992). The Comparative Costs of Community Service and Custody in Scotland. *Howard Journal*, *31*, pp. 8–30.

Knott, C. (2004). Evidence-based Practice in the National Probation Service. In R. Burnett and C. Roberts (Eds), *What Works in Probation and Youth Justice: Developing Evidence-Based Practice* (pp. 14–28). Cullompton: Willan.

Kogan, M. (1999). The Impact of Research on Policy. In Coffield, M. (Ed.), *Speaking Truth to Power: Research and Policy on Lifelong Learning* (pp. 11–18). Bristol: Polity Press.

Labour Party. (1996). *Tackling Youth Crime: Reforming Youth Justice* (TYCRYJ). London: Labour Party.

Lasor, W., Hubbard, D. and Bush, F. (1996). *Old Testament Survey: The Message, Form and Background of the Old Testament*. Grand Rapids: Eerdmans.

DOI: 10.1057/9781137400468.0010

Lewis, S., Maguire, M., Raynor, P., Vanstone, M. and Vennard, J. (2007). What Works in Resettlement? Findings from Seven Pathfinders for Short-Term Prisoners in England and Wales, *Criminology and Criminal Justice, 7*(1), pp. 33–53.

Likert, R. (1932). A Technique for the Measurement of Attitudes. *Archives of Psychology;* No.140.

Lipsey, M.W. (1992). Juvenile Delinquency Treatment: A Meta-Analytic Inquiry into the Variability of Effects. In T. D. Cook, H. Cooper. and D. S. Cordray (Eds), *Meta-analysis for Explanation: A Casebook* (pp. 83–127). New York: Russell Sage Foundation.

Lipsey, M. W. (1995). What Do We Learn from 400 Studies on the Effectiveness of Treatment with Juvenile Delinquents? In J. Mcguire (Ed.), What *Works: Reducing Re-Offending: Guidelines from Research and Practice.* Chichester: Wiley.

Lipsey, M. W., Chapman, G. L. and Landenberger, N. A. (2001). Cognitive-Behavioural Programs for Offenders. *Annals of the American Academy of Political and Social Science, 578*, pp. 144–157.

Lipsey, M., Landenberger, N. and Wilson, S. (2007). *Effects of Cognitive-Behavioral Programs for Criminal Offenders – Campbell Collaboration Systematic Review.* Vanderbilt Institute for Public Social Policy: Center for Evaluation Research and Methodology.

Lloyd, C., Mair, G. and Hough, M. (1994). *Explaining Reconviction Rates: A Critical Analysis.* Home Office. Research Study 136, London: Home Office.

Mair, G. (1997). Community Penalties and the Probation Service. In M. Maguire, R. Morgan and R. Reiner (Eds), *Oxford Handbook of Criminology* (2nd edition) Oxford: Clarendon Press.

Mair, G. and H. Mills. (2009). *The Community Order and the Suspended Sentence Order Three Years On: The Views and Experiences of Probation Officers and Offenders.* Retrieved from: http://www.crimeandjustice. org.uk/communitysentences.Html.

Mair, G., Cross, N. and Taylor, S. (2007). *The Use and Impact of the Community Order and the Suspended Sentence Order.* London: Centre for Crime and Justice Studies.

Mair, G. and May, C. (1997). *Offenders on Probation.* Home Office Research Study 167. London: Home Office.

Marshall, T. (1999). *Restorative Justice: An Overview.* London: Home Office.

DOI: 10.1057/9781137400468.0010

Maruna, S. (2001). *Making Good: How Ex-convicts Reform and Rebuild their Lives*. Washington DC: American Psychological Association.

Maruna, S. and King, A. (2008), Selling the Public on Probation: Beyond the Bib, *The Journal of Community and Criminal Justice*, 55(4), pp. 337–351.

Matza, D. (1969). *Becoming Deviant*. Englewood Cliffs, NJ: Prentice-Hall.

May, C. (1999). *Explaining Reconviction Following Community Sentences: The Role of Social Factors*. Home Office Research Study 192, London: Home Office.

McCold, P. and Wachtel, T. (2003). *In Pursuit of Paradigm: A Theory of Restorative Justice*. Paper Presented at the XIII World Congress of Criminology, Rio de Janeiro, Brazil. Retrieved from: http://www.iirp. org/pdf/paradigm.pdf.

McCulloch, T. (2010). Exploring Community Service: Understanding Compliance. In McNeill, F., Raynor, P. and Trotter, C (Eds), *Offender Supervision: New Directions in Theory, Research and Practice* (pp. 228–236). Cullompton: Willan.

McGagh, M. (2007). *Community Service: An Exploration of the Views of Community Service Supervisors in the Irish Probation Service*. Retrieved from: http://www.probation.ie/pws/websitepublishing. nsf/AttachmentsByTitle/An+exploration+of+the+views+of+Com munity+Service+Supervisors+in+the+Irish+Probation+Service+- +Aug+07/$FILE/An+exploration+of+the+views+of+Community+Se rvice+Supervisors+in+the+Irish+Probation+Service+-+Aug+07.pdf.

McGuire, J. (Ed.). (1995). *What Works: Reduce Re-offending – Guidelines from Research and Practice*. Chichester: Wiley.

McIvor, G. (1991). Community Service Work Placements. *The Howard Journal, 30*, pp. 19–29.

McIvor, G. (1992). *Sentenced to Serve*. Burlington: Ashgate.

McIvor, G. (1993). Community Service by Offenders: Agency Experiences and Attitudes. *Research on Social Work Practice, 3*, 66–82.

McIvor, G. (2002). *What Works in Community Service?* CJSW Briefing Paper 6. Edinburgh: Criminal Justice Social Work Development Centre.

McIvor, G. (2010). *30 Years of Unpaid Work by Offenders in Scotland*. Retrieved from http://www.ejprob.ro/uploads_ro/702/Paying_ back_30_years_of_unpaid_work_by_offenders_in_Scotland.pdf.

McIvor, G. and M. Barry (1998). *Social Work and Criminal Justice – Volume 6:Probation*. Edinburgh: Stationery Office.

DOI: 10.1057/9781137400468.0010

McIvor, G. and Barry, M. (2000). *Social Work and Criminal Justice: Volume 8 – The Longer-term Effectiveness of Supervision*, Edinburgh: Scottish Executive Central Research Unit.

McNeill, F. (2006). Community Supervision: Context and Relationships Matter. In: B.Goldson and J. Muncie (Eds), *Youth Crime and Justice* (pp.125–138). London: SAGE.

McNutt, H. (2010). *Tainted by the James Bulger Legacy: Why Does the Horrific Murder of a Merseyside Toddler by Two Young Boys in 1993 Still Have Such a Lasting Effect on the Way We Demonise and Stereotype Disturbed Children?* Retrieved from: http://www.guardian.co.uk/society/2010/mar/03/james-bulger-legacy-disturbed-children.

McSweeney, T., Stevens, A., Hunt, N. and Turnbull, P. J. (2006). Twisting Arms or a Helping Hand? Assessing the Impact of Coerced and Comparable Voluntary Drug Treatment Options. *British Journal of Criminology*, 47(3), pp. 470–490.

Melossi, D. and Pavarini, M. (1981). *The Prison and the Factory*. London: Macmillan.

Menard, S. (2002). *Applied Logistic Regression Analysis* (2nd edition). Thousand Oaks: Sage.

Mercier, C. and Alarie, S. (2002). Pathways out of Deviance: Implications for Programme Evaluation. In S. Brochu, C. Da Agra and M. M. Cousinaeu (Eds), *Drugs and Crime Deviant Pathways* (pp. 229–239). Aldershot: Ashgate.

Merrington, S. and Stanley, S. (2000). Doubts about the What Works Initiative, *Probation Journal*, 47(3), pp. 272–275.

Milaniam, K. (2009). *Verbal Abuse Forces Suspension of Hi-Vis 'Community Payback' Jackets*. Retrieved from: http://www.kentonline.co.uk/kentonline/newsarchive.aspx?articleid=54672.

Miller, G. A. (1956). The Magic Number Seven, Plus or Minus Two: Some Limits on Capacity for Processing Information. *Psychological Review*, 63, pp. 81–97.

Ministry of Justice. (2010). *Unpaid work / Community Payback: Service Specification for Community Payback*. Retrieved from: http://www.justice.gov.uk/downloads/offenders/probation-instructions/pi_02_2010_unpaid_work_community_payback_service_specification.pdf/.

Ministry of Justice. (2011a). *Re-Offending of Juveniles: Results from the 2009 Cohort*. London: Ministry of Justice.

DOI: 10.1057/9781137400468.0010

Ministry of Justice. (2011b). *Adult Reconvictions: Results from the 2009 Cohort*. London: Ministry of Justice.

Ministry of Justice. (2012a). *Youth Justice Board*. Retrieved from http://www.justice.gov.uk/about/yjb/index.htm.

Ministry of Justice. (2012b). *Punishment and Reform: Effective Community Sentences*. London: TSO.

Ministry of Justice. (2012c). *About Her Majesty's Inspectorate of Probation*. Retrieved from: http://www.justice.gov.uk/about/hmi-probation.

Ministry of Justice. (2012d). *2012 Compendium of Re-Offending Statistics and Analysis*. London: Ministry of Justice.

Ministry of Justice. (2015a). Offender Management Statistics Quarterly: January to March 2015. Retrieved from: https://www.gov.uk/government/statistics/offender-management-statistics-quarterly-january-to-march-2015.

Ministry of Justice. (2015b). Youth Justice Annual Statistics: 2013 to 2014. Retrieved from: https://www.gov.uk/government/statistics/youth-justice-annual-statistics-2013-to-2014.

Moore, R. (2007). Adult Offenders' Perceptions of Their Underlying Problems: Findings from the OASYS Self Assessment Questionnaire. Home Office Findings 284. Development and Statistics Directorate. London: Home Office.

Mulvey, E. P., Arthur, M. W. and Reppucci, N. D. (1993). The Prevention and Treatment of Juvenile Delinquency: A Review of the Research. *Clinical Psychology Review. 13*, pp. 133–167.

Muncie, J. (1999). Institutionalised Intolerance: Youth Justice and the 1998 Crime and Disorder Act. *Critical Social Policy, 19*(2), pp. 147–175.

Muncie, J. (2004). *Youth and Crime* (2nd edition). London: Sage.

Muncie, J., Hughes, G. and E, McLaughlin. (Eds), (2002). *Youth Justice: Critical Readings*. London: Sage.

Murray, J. and Farrington, D. P. (2005). Parental Imprisonment: Effects on Boys Antisocial Behaviour and Delinquency through the Life-Course. *Journal of Child Psychology and Psychiatry, 46*, pp. 1269–78.

National Probation Service. (2005). *Probation Circular: Visible Unpaid Work*. Retrieved from: http://www.probation.homeoffice.gov.uk/files/pdf/PC66%202005.pdf.

NACRO. (2005). *Safer Society Magazine* (Issue 25). London: NACRO.

NAPO. (2010). *Threats, Lack of Training and Unrealistic Expectations of Unpaid Work* (Press Release). London: NAPO.

DOI: 10.1057/9781137400468.0010

NAPO. (2008). *Call for Withdrawal of Distinctive Clothing for Community Payback*. Retrieved from: http://www.napo.org.uk/cgi-bin/dbman/db. cgi?db=default&uid=default&ID=189&view_records=1&ww=1.

NAPO. (2009). *High Visibility Vests: Threats, Abuse, Boycotts and Legal Issues*. Retrieved from: http://www.napo.org.uk/cgi-bin/dbman/db.cg i?db=default&uid=default&ID=191&view_records=1&ww=1.

Natale, L. (2010). Youth Crime in England and Wales. Retrieved from: http://www.civitas.org.uk/crime/factsheet-youthoffending.pdf.

Nee, C. (2004). The Offender's Perspective on Crime: Methods and Principles in Data Collection. In A. Needs and G. Towl (Eds), *Applying Psychology to Forensic Practice* (pp. 3–18). London: BPS Blackwell.

Nescot Report. (2007). *Opening Doors: Research Reports 2007*. Surrey: Nescot College.

Newburn, T. (1998). Tackling Youth Crime and Reforming Youth Justice: The Origins and Nature of New Labour Policy. *Policy Studies*, 19(3/4), pp. 199–212.

Newburn, T. (2007). *Criminology*. Cullompton: Willan Publishing.

Newburn, T., Crawford, A., Earle, R., Goldie, S., Hale, C., Hallam, A., Masters, G., Netten, A., Saunders, R., Sharpe, K. and Uglow, S. (2002). *The Introduction of Referral Orders into the Youth Justice System: Final Report* (Home Office Research Study 242). London, Home Office.

Niven, S. and Stewart, D. (2005). *Resettlement Outcomes on Release from Prison in 2003*. Home Office Findings 248. Retrieved from: www. homeoffice.gov.uk/rds/pdfs05/r248.pdf.

Noakes, L. and Wincup, E. (2004). *Criminological Research: Understanding QualitativeMethods*. London: Sage.

Nutley, S., Davies, H. T. O. and Tilley, N. (2000). Editorial: Getting Research into Practice. *Public Money and Management*, 20(4), pp. 3–6.

O'Malley, P. (2001). Risk, Crime and Prudentialism Revisited. In K. Stenson and R. Sullivan (Eds), *Crime, Risk and Justice: The Politics of Crime Control in Liberal Democracies* (pp.83–103). Devon: Willan.

Palmer, T. (1992). *The Re-Emergence of Correctional Intervention*. Newbury Park, CA: SAGE.

Pamment, N. (2010). Youth Offending Teams: A Multi-Agency Success or System Failure? In A. Pycroft and D. Gough (Eds), *Multi Agency Working in Criminal Justice: Control and Care in Contemporary Correctional Practice* (pp. 219–232). Bristol. Policy Press.

DOI: 10.1057/9781137400468.0010

Pamment, N. and Ellis, T. (2010). A Retrograde Step: The Potential Impact of High Visibility Uniforms in Youth Justice. *Howard Journal, 49*(1), pp. 18–30.

Pease, K. (1980). A Brief History of Community Service. In K. Pease and W. McWilliams (Eds), *Community Service by Order*. Scotland: Scottish Academic Press.

Pease, K. (1985). Community Service Orders. In M. Tonry and N. Morris (Eds), *Crime and Justice*. Chicago: University of Chicago Press.

Pease, K., Billingham, S. and Earnshaw. J. (1977). *Community Service Assessed in 1976*. Home Office Research Study 39. London: HMSO.

Pease, K. Durkin, P. Earnshaw, I. and Thorpe, J. (1975). *Community Service Orders*. Home Office Research Study No. 29. London: HMSO.

Pemberton, C. (2010). *Youth Justice: Reparation Orders for Young Offenders on the Rise*. Retrieved from: http://www.communitycare.co.uk/blogs/childrens-services-blog/2010/01/youth-justice-reparation-orders-for-young-offenders-on-the-rise.html.

Petersilia, J. (2005). Hard Time: Ex-Offenders Returning Home after Prison. *Corrections Today, 67*, pp. 66–72.

Raynor, P. (1998). Attitudes, Social Problems and Reconvictions in the STOP Probation Experiment. *Howard Journal, 37*, pp.1–15.

Raynor, P. and Vanstone M. (1996). 'Reasoning and Rehabilitation in Britain: The Results of the Straight Thinking on Probation (STOP) Programme', *International Journal of Offender Therapy and Comparative Criminology, 40*(4), pp. 272–284.

Raynor, P. and Vanstone, M. (2002). *Understanding Community Penalties*. Buckingham: Open University Press.

Reddy, B. (1991). Community Service Orders: An alternative Sentence. *Singapore Academy Law Journal, 3*, pp. 230–237.

Rethinking Crime and Punishment. (2005). *Unlocking Learning: Examining Public and Professional Attitudes towards the Role of Education in Relation to Crime and Punishment of Young Offenders*. Retrieved from: http://www.rethinking.org.uk/informed/Unlocking%20learning.pdf.

Rex, S. (1999). Desistance from Offending: Experiences of Probation. *The Howard Journal of Criminal Justice, 38*, pp. 366–383.

Rex, S. (2001). Beyond Cognitive-Behaviouralism? Reflections on the Effectiveness Literature. In A. Bottoms, L. Gelsthorpe and S. Rex (Eds), *Community Penalties: Change and challenges* (pp.67–87). Cullompten: Willan.

DOI: 10.1057/9781137400468.0010

Rex, S. and Gelsthorpe, L. (2002). The Role of Community Service in Reducing Offending: Evaluating Pathfinder Projects in the UK, *The Howard Journal*, 41(4), pp. 311–325.

Rex, S., Gelsthorpe, L., Roberts, C. and Jordan, P. (2003). *Crime Reduction Programme: An Evaluation of Community Service Pathfinder Projects: Final Report 2002* (RDS Occasional Paper 87). London: Home Office.

Robinson, G. and Shapland, J. (2008). Reducing Recidivism: A Task for Restorative Justice? *British Journal of Criminology*, 48(3), pp. 337–358.

Robinson, G. (2002). Exploring Risk Management in Probation Practice. *Punishment and Society*, 4, pp. 5–25.

Robson, C. (2002). *Real World Research: A Resource for Social Scientists and Practitioner-Researchers* (2nd edition). Oxford: Blackwell.

Roche, D. (2001). The Evolving Definition of Restorative Justice. *Contemporary Justice Review*, 43(3–4), pp. 341–353.

Rogowski, S. (2010). Young Offending: Towards a Radical/Critical Social Policy, *Journal of Youth Studies* 13(2), pp. 197–211.

Roper, M. (2008). *Community Service Offenders Forced to Wear New Hi-Vis 'Vest of Shame'*. Retrieved from: http://www.mirror.co.uk/.

Ross, R. R. and Fabiano, E. (1985). *Time to Think: A Cognitive Model of Delinquency Prevention and Offender Rehabilitation*. Tennessee: Institute of Social Sciences and Arts, Inc.

Rutter, M., Giller, H. and Hagell, A. (1998). *Antisocial Behaviour by Young People*. Cambridge: Cambridge University Press.

Sampson, R. J. and Laub, J. (1993). *Crime in the Making: Pathways and Turning Points through Life*. Cambridge, MA: Harvard University Press.

Sanders, A. (1998). What Principles Underlie Criminal Justice Policy in the 1990s? *Oxford Journal of Legal Studies*, 18(3), pp. 533–542.

Sarno, C., Hough, M., Nee, C. and Herrington, V. (1999). *A Study of Two Probation Employment Schemes in Inner London and Surrey*. Home Office Research Findings No.136. London: Home Office.

Schiff, M. (1999). The Impact of Restorative Interventions on Juvenile Offenders. In G. Bazemore and L. Walgrave (Eds), *Restorative Juvenile Justice: Repairing the Harm of Youth Crime*. New York: Criminal Justice Press.

Scottish Executive. (2001). *Reconvictions of Offenders Discharged from Custody or Given Non-custodial Sentences in 1995*. Scotland, Edinburgh: Scottish Executive Statistical Services.

DOI: 10.1057/9781137400468.0010

Scottish Executive. (2003). *Reconvictions of Offenders Discharged from Custody or Given Non-custodial Sentences in 1997*. Edinburgh: Criminal Justice Series.

Shaw, J. and Cantrell, H. (2008). *Improving the Employability of Offenders – Working Brief* (issue 194). London: CESI.

Shepherd, A. and Whiting, E. (2006). *Re-Offending of Adults: Results from the 2003 Cohort (Report 20/06)*. London: Home Office.

Sherman, L. and Strang, H. (2007). *Restorative Justice: The Evidence.* Retrieved from: http://www.esmeefairbairn.org.uk/docs/RJ_exec_summary.pdf.

Sherman, L., Gottfredson, D., MacKenzie, D., Eck, J., Reuter, P. and Bushway, S. (1997). *Preventing Crime: What Works, What Doesn't, What's Promising*. Washington: US Department of Justice.

Social Exclusion Unit. (2002). *Reducing Re-offending by Ex-prisoners.* London: Office of the Deputy Prime Minister.

Smith, D. (2003). New Labour and Youth Justice. *Children and Society,* *17*, pp. 226–235.

Solomon, E. and Silvestri A. (2008). *Community Sentences Digest* (2nd edition). London: Centre for Crime and Justice Studies.

Souhami, A. (2007). Multi-agency Working: Experiences in the Youth Justice System. In S. Green., E. Lacaster and S. Feasey (Eds), *Addressing Offending Behaviour* (pp. 208–229). Cullompton: Willan.

Spicer, K. and Glicksman, A. (2004). *Adult Reconviction: Results from the 2001 Cohort*. London: Home Office.

Stanley, C. (2001). Will New Youth Justice Work? *Probation Journal, 48*, pp. 93–101.

Stanley, S. (2007). *The Use of the Community Order and the Suspended Sentence Order for Young Adult Offenders*. London: Centre for Crime and Justice Studies.

Stenner, P. and Taylor, D. (2008). Psychosocial Welfare; Reflections on an Emerging Field, *Critical and Social Policy, 28*(4), pp.415–437.

Straw, J. and Michael, A. (1996). *Tackling Youth Crime: Reforming Youth Justice*. London: Labour Party.

Stephenson, M., Giller, H. and Brown, S. (2007). *Effective Practice in Youth Justice*. Cullompton: Devon.

Sumner, M. (2006). Reparation. In E. McLaughlin and J. Muncie (Eds), *The Sage Dictionary of Criminology* (pp. 351–352). London: Sage.

Sutton, P. (2010). *Unpaid Work by 16 &17 Year Olds: A Feasibility Study for YJB, NOMS and YJPU*. London: YJB.

DOI: 10.1057/9781137400468.0010

Tallant, C., Sambrook, M. and Green, S. (2008). Engagement Skills: Best Practice or Effective Practice? In S. Green, E. Lancaster and S. Feasey (Eds), *Addressing Offending Behaviour: Context, Practice and Values* (pp. 75–92). Devon, UK: Willan.

Tonry, M. and Petersilia, J. (1999). American Prisons. In M. Tonry and J. Petersilia (Eds), *Prisons*. Chicago: University of Chicago Press.

Travis, A. (2011). *Public Sector Cuts: Rise in Youth Crime Feared as Key Teams Are Reduced.* Retrieved from: http://www.guardian.co.uk/society/2011/mar/25/public-sector-cuts-youth-crime.

Travis, A. (2007). *Prison Suicides Up to Two a Week as Jail Numbers Soar.* Retrieved from http://www.guardian.co.uk/uk/2007/jun/13/prisonsandprobation.ukcrime.

Trotter, C. (1993). *The Supervision of Offenders: What Works?* Melbourne: Victoria Office of Corrections.

Trotter, C. (1999). *Working with Involuntary Clients*, London: Sage.

United Kingdom Council for Graduate Education (2002). *Professional Doctorates.* Dudley: UKCGE.

Utting, D. and Vennard, J. (2000). *What Works with Young Offenders in the Community?* Ilford: Barnado's.

Varah, M. (1981). What about the Workers? Offenders on Community Service Orders Express Their Opinions. *Probation Journal*, pp. 120–123.

Vaughan, B. (2000). The Government of Youth: Disorder and Dependence? *Social and Legal Studies*, 9(3), pp. 347–366.

Von Hirsch, A. (1993). *Censure and Sanctions.* Oxford: Oxford University Press.

Von Hirsch, A. and Ashworth, A. (Eds), (1998). *Principled Sentencing* (2nd edition). Oxford: Hart Publishing.

Walgrave, L. (1999). Community Service as a Cornerstone of a Systemic Restorative Response to (Juvenile) Crime. In G. Bazemore and L. Walgrave (Eds), *Restorative Juvenile Justice: Repairing the Harm of Youth Crime* (pp. 129–154). Monsey, NY: Criminal Justice Press.

Wasik, M. (2008). The Legal Framework. In S. Green, E. Lancaster and S. Feasey (Eds), *Addressing Offending Behavior: Context, Practice and Values* (pp. 3–24). Cullompton: Willan.

Wasik, M. and Von Hirsch, A. (1988). Non-Custodial Penalties and the Principles of Desert, *The Criminal Law Review*, pp. 555–572.

DOI: 10.1057/9781137400468.0010

Whiting, E. and Cuppleditch, L. (2006). *Re-Offending of Juveniles: Results from the 2004 Cohort*. Home Office Online Report 10/06. London: Home Office.

Wilson, D. (2006). Some Reflections on Researching with Young Black People and the Youth Justice System. *Youth Justice*, 6(3), pp. 181–193.

Wilcox, A. and Hoyle, C. (2004). *The National Evaluation of the Youth Justice Board's Restorative Justice Projects*. London: YJB.

Wilson, D. and Wahidin, A. (2006). 'Real Work' in Prison: Absences, *Obstacles and Opportunities*. Centre for Criminal Justice Policy and Research, UCE in Birmingham. Retrieved from: http://www.lhds.uce.ac.uk/criminaljustice/docs/Real_Work_Report.pdf.

Woolf. H. and Tumin, S. (1991). *Prison Disturbances April 1990*. London: HMISO.

Work Foundation. (2010). *Employability and Skills in the UK: Redefining theDebate*. Retrieved from: http://www.theworkfoundation.com/Assets/Docs/LCCI-CET%20Future%20Skills%20Policy%20FINAL%2001%2011%2010.pdf.

Worrall, A. (1997). *Punishment in the Community: The Future of Criminal Justice*. London/New York: Addison Wesley Longman.

Worrall, A. and Hoy, C. (2005). *Punishment in the Community: Managing Offenders, Making Choices* (2nd edition), Cullompton: Willan Publishing.

Young, W. (1979). *Community Service Orders: The Development and Use of a New Penal Measure*. London: Heinemann.

YJB. (2000). *The Crime and Disorder Act Guidance Document: Reparation Order*. London: YJB.

YJB. (2002). *The National Specification for Learning and Skills: For Young People on a Detention and Training Order in Prison Service Accommodation*. London: Youth Justice Board.

YJB. (2006). *Developing Restorative Justice: An Action Plan*. Retrieved from: http://www.yjb.gov.uk/publications/Resources/Downloads/RJ%20Action%20Plan.pdf.

YJB. (2008). *To Develop and Improve Reparation, as Part of the Youth Crime Action Plan. Good Practice for Youth Offending Teams (YOTs)*. Retrieved from http://www.yjb.gov.uk/NR/rdonlyres/511B3C1D-176A-4EA9-8535-93B2411753F7/0/TodevelopandimprovereparationaspartoftheYouthCrimeActionPlan.pdf.

DOI: 10.1057/9781137400468.0010

YJB. (2009a). *Youth Justice System: Youth Offending Teams – Who Are They? What Do They Do?* Retrieved from: http://www.yjb.gov.uk/en-gb/yjs/YouthOffendingTeams/.

YJB. (2009b). *Courts and Orders: The Criminal Justice and Immigration Act.* Retrieved from http://www.yjb.gov.uk/en-gb/practitioners/CourtsAndOrders/CriminalJusticeandImmigrationAct/.

YJB. (2009c). *YJB Corporate and Business Plan 2009/10.* Retrieved from: http://www.yjb.gov.uk/publications/Scripts/prodView.asp?idproduct=449&eP.

YJB. (2010). *Making Good.* Retrieved from: http://www.yjb.gov.uk/en-gb/yjs/MakingGood/.

YJB. (2011). *Reparation Order.* Retrieved from: http://www.justice.gov.uk/youth-justice/courts-and-orders/disposals/reparation-order.

Zedner, L. (1994). Reparation and Retribution: Are They Reconcilable? *The Modern Law Review, 57*, pp. 228–250.

Zedner, L. (2002). Dangers of Dystopias in Penal Theory. *Oxford Journal of Legal Studies, 22*(2), pp. 341–366.

DOI: 10.1057/9781137400468.0010

Index

Note: 'f' indicates figure, 'n' indicates note, 't' indicates table.

Actual Bodily Harm (ABH), 57
adult community service (CS),
    3, 6, 15, 27n1, 30, 53,
    76, 82
  media representation of,
    17–18
  positive and negative
    practices in unpaid
    work, 52–54, 53t
  post 2000, 16–21
  as punishment, 11, 25
  as re-integrative alternative
    to custody, 8–10, see also
    re-integrative benefits
    of CS
  renaming of, 16, see also
    unpaid work
  statistics of use of, 9–10
  studies into, see studies into
    adult CS
  see also Community Service
    Orders (CSOs)
adult offender(s)
  CPO for, 30
  CSO for, 8, 17
  opinions of community
    service, 40–42, 43–44t,
    45
  reconviction rates of, 31–37
  skills gained by, 40–45
  unpaid work for, 27n2, see
    also unpaid work

    see also adult community
      service (CS); studies
      into adult CS
Advisory Council on the Penal
    System, 8–9, 11, 23, 25,
    26, 34, 66, 76
Angus, S., 11, 12
Anti-Social Behaviour Orders
    (ASBOs), 14–15
ASSET, 5, 6n2, 48t, 58
Audit Commission, 13, 14

beneficiaries, contact with, 2,
    24, 38t, 41–42, 41t, 46,
    53t, 54, 69–70, 77f, 78,
    79, 81
Bottoms, A., 12, 14, 18, 27n9, 46
Braithwaite, J., 2
Brown, S., 20, 21, 23, 26, 72, 76
Bulger, J., 11, 12, 13
Bulger killing, 11–12
Bush, F., 8

Casey, L., 15–18, 25, 26, 76, 81
Casey review, 17
Cognitive Behavioural Therapy
    (CBT), 22
combination orders, 11, 25,
    27n5, 33–34, 34t
Community Payback, 16–18, 25,
    26, 76
  see also vests of shame

Community Punishment Order
  (CPO), 15t, 16, 25, 27n12, 30, 31t,
  35, 36t
Community Order (CO), 15t, 16, 25,
  27n2
community reparation
  impact on young offenders, 47–52,
    59–66, 68–71, *see also* studies
    into YJCR
  influence on adult offenders, 40–46,
    see also studies into adult CS
  offender/staff interaction, 65–66
  and problem solving, *see* problem
    solving
  purpose of, 2–4
  research approach, 4–6
  and restorative justice, 20–21
  types of placement, 58–59, *see also*
    work placements
  see also adult community service
    (CS); unpaid work; youth
    justice community reparation
    (YJCR); Youth Offending Team
    (YOT)
Community Reparation Orders
  (CROs), 44–46, 55n3
Community Service Orders (CSOs)
  definition of, 8
  implementation of, 9
  objective of, 8–9
  renaming of, 16, 25, *see also*
    Community Punishment Order
    (CPO)
  probation statistics of, 10
  and reconviction rates, 30–37, *see also*
    reconviction/reconviction rates
  stand alone, 30
Conservative Party, 12, 13
Crime and Disorder Act (CDA) (1998),
  11, 14–15, 25, 46, 49, 76
Crime Concern, 50
Criminal Justice Act (CJA)
  1972, 9
  1991, 10–13, 25
  1993, 12
  2003, 16, 30

Criminal Justice and Immigration Act
  (2008), 18
Criminal Justice and Public Order Act
  (1994), 12
Crown Prosecution Service (CPS), 30
curfew, 10, 14, 19t, 27n8, 27n12, 35,
  36–37t
Curfew and Child Safety Orders
  (CCSOs), 14–15
Curran, J., 39t, 44–46, 53t, 59,
  62, 63, 65, 66, 68, 69, 77,
  78, 80
custodial sentence, *see* custody
custody, 8–10, 12, 15t, 17, 19t, 23,
  25, 30, 31t, 32, 33t, 34, 35, 40,
  58, 81
  alternative to, 8–10, 25, 34
  see also incarceration

decorating, 2, 23, 38t, 40, 59, 59t, 60,
  61t, 73
Delens-Ravier, I., 54–55
desistance from crime, 2, 20, 21,
  27, 61, 62, 68, 70, 73, 77f,
  79, 81
disposals, 3, 4, 6, 12, 21, 25–27, 58, 62,
  70, 73
  criminal justice, 30–32, 33t
  first-tier, 15, 18, *see also*
    Reparation Order (RO);
    Referral Order
  offender characteristics against,
    34–35, 34t
  reconviction rates and, 31–35, 46–47,
    47t, 50–52, 54
  re-integrative potential of, 41, 42,
    67–68, 76–78, 80–82
  sentencing framework, 1998, 15t
Dugmore, P., 12–14, 20, 28n13

employability skills, acquisition of, 2, 3,
  21–24, 26–27, 42, 45, 59–63, 70,
  73, 77f, 78–81
  see also work placements
Enhanced Community Punishment
  (ECP), 16

Gelsthorpe, L., 9–11, 16, 21, 23–26, 31, 37, 42, 43, 52, 54–55, 65–66, 70, 76, 78, 80
Giller, H., 20–23, 26, 73, 76
graffiti removal, 2, 45
Grieve, D., 18

HM Inspectorate of Probation (HMIP), 23, 78, 79, 81
Holdaway, S., 3, 15, 18, 20, 21, 23, 24, 26, 48t, 49–52, 53t, 54, 57–59, 63, 66, 70, 71, 76–79
Howard, M. (Home Secretary), 12
Hoyle, C., 3, 20, 26, 30, 48t, 49–50, 51t, 52, 53t, 54, 57–59, 63, 66, 68, 70, 71, 77–79
Hubbard, D., 8
Hughes, G., 11

incarceration, 8, 9, 32, 40, 47
   see also custody
Intensive Supervision and Surveillance (ISS), 4, 81, 82
Intensive Supervision and Surveillance Programme (ISSP), 4, 18, 48t, 51, 57

Jennings, D., 46–47, 77, 79

'kindling preparation', 59t, 59, 67, 70, 78
King, M., 17, 18, 25, 26, 40, 76

Labour Party, 12, 13, 25
Lasor, W., 8
litter picking, 2, 38t, 45, 48t, 52, 53t, 59, 60, 62, 67, 69, 70, 71, 78
Lloyd, C., 30–35, 42, 52, 55n1, 77

'*Making Good*', 2, 18, 20, 26
Maruna, S., 17, 18, 21, 24, 25, 26, 76
May, C., 22, 23, 33–35, 42, 52, 77
McIvor, G., 17–18, 23–26, 27n1, 31–32, 37, 38t, 40–42, 45–46, 52, 53t, 54, 55n2, 59, 62–63, 65, 66, 68–71, 73, 76–80

McLaughlin, E., 11
McMahon, W., 20
menial activities, 3, 38t, 39t, 40, 45, 48t, 49, 50, 52, 53t, 59–63, 65–69, 71–73, 77–80
   see also 'kindling preparation'; litter picking; shrub clearance
Muncie, J., 11, 13, 14, 25, 76

National Association of Probation Officers (NAPO), 9, 17, 25
Non-custodial and Semi-custodial Penalties, 8

offence seriousness/offender seriousness, 10, 31, 34, 35, 46
offender(s)
   adult, *see* adult offender(s)
   attitudes to work placements, 41–42, 41t, 49, 59–63, 61t
   and beneficiaries, 2, 24, 38t, 41–42, 41t, 46, 53t, 54, 69–70, 77f, 78, 79, 81
   characteristics, 31–32, 33t, 34t, 35, 38t, 46, 57
   female, 60, 64, 68, 71, 72
   male, 34t, 38t, 39t, 46, 47t, 48t, 49, 50, 57, 60–61, 64, 67–73
   and restorative justice, 21
   seriousness, 10, 31, 34, 35, 46
   unemployed, 9, 76
   unpaid work for, *see* unpaid work
   work placements for, *see* work placements
   young, *see* young offender(s)

painting, 2, 23, 59, 59t, 60, 61t, 71, 73
Pathfinder projects, 39t, 42–44, 43t
   see also pro-social modelling (PSM); tackling other offending-related needs (TON)
Pettit, P., 2
Pickford, J., 11, 12
Police National Computer (PNC), 50
populist punitiveness, 11, 12–13
principle of proportionality, 10

prison population, 8, 9, 10, 12

probation, 6, 9–11, 14, 24, 25, 27n5, 31t, 33t, 33–35, 36t, 42, 78, 81, 82
  see also probation officers; probation orders; probation service

probation officers, 9, 11
  see also National Association of Probation Officers (NAPO)

probation orders, 30, 32

probation service, 10–11, 16, 27n9, 33, 40, 82

problem solving, 2, 6, 16, 23, 53t, 63–66, 68, 77f, 78, 81

pro-social modelling (PSM), 16, 23–24, 39t, 42, 44, 45, 53t, 65, 66, 79

punishment, 3, 6, 8, 10–12, 15t, 20, 25, 26, 48t, 50, 51, 52, 53t, 66–68, 76, 79
  see also Community Punishment Order (CPO); punitive/ punitiveness

punitive/punitiveness, 2, 8, 11–12, 16, 17, 25, 27n10, 66, 68, 69–70, 76, 79

questionnaires, 5, 38–39t, 40–44, 48t, 59, 60, 67, 68, 72, 74

recidivism
  positive impact upon, 31, 37
  prevention of, 21, 76
  reduction in, 22, 24, 42, 77
  see also reconviction/reconviction rates; re-offending

reconviction/reconviction rates, 3–4, 6
  actual and predicted, 34–35, 35t
  in adults
    1983–2003, 30–31, 31t
    2001 Cohort, 35–36, 36t
  community penalties and custody, 32–33, 33t
  effect of community service on, 42, 44
  offender characteristics
    in males, 33–34, 34t
    within disposal groups, 32, 33t
  by requirement type, 35–37, 36–37t

by restorative intervention type, 50–51, 51t
  in youth, 46–47, 47t

Referral Order, 15, 15t, 18, 19t, 30, 57, 57f

rehabilitation, 4, 6, 11, 16, 25–26, 27n10, 28n13, 36, 37, 47, 63, 65
  see also Youth Rehabilitation Order (YRO)

re-integrative benefits of CS, 2, 9, 11, 16, 18, 25–26, 37, 40–46, 63–66, 68–70, 76–78, 77f

re-offending, 6n2, 30, 35, 39t, 46, 47, 58
  attitudes toward, 72–74
  effect of community service on, 42, 44
  reduction in, 2, 21, 22, 27, 42, 44, 45, 49, 63, 71, 76, 78, 79, 81, 82
  see also recidivism; reconviction/ reconviction rates

reparation, 2, 17
  see also community reparation; youth justice community reparation (YJCR)

Reparation Order (RO), 3–4, 15, 18, 19t, 30, 44, 46–49, 47t, 48t, 52, 57, 57f, 79

restorative justice (RJ), 3, 20–21, 23, 24, 49–51, 48t, 57

retribution, 6, 10, 17, 21, 25–26, 76, 79

Rex, S., 3, 9–11, 16, 21, 23–26, 31, 37, 39t, 42–44, 46, 52–55, 62, 63, 65, 66, 68, 70, 73, 76–78, 80

Scotland, 27n1, 38t, 39t, 40–42

sentencing framework, 10, 15, 15t, 18, 19t

shrub clearance, 3, 49, 52, 53t, 59, 63, 67, 70, 78

social isolation, 9, 76

Stephenson, M., 21, 23, 24, 26, 76

Straw, J. (Home Secretary), 13

studies into adult CS, 37, 38–39t
  evaluation of CROs, 44–46
  Pathfinder projects, 39t, 42–44, 43t
  in Scotland, 40–42, 41t
  in Warwickshire, 40

studies into YJCR, 48t
  assessment of the pilot YOTs, 49
  evaluation of ISSP, 51–52
  'local' evaluation of YOT projects, 51
  restorative justice interventions of
    YJB, 49–51
supervisor(s), 4, 9, 23, 24, 39t, 45, 49,
    55, 59, 61–63, 65–69, 71–74, 77,
    79–81
  see also work placements,
    supervisors' opinion of

tackling other offending-related needs
    (TON), 42, 44
Trotter, C., 23, 24, 65, 66, 79

unpaid work, 2, 4, 6, 15
  by CSO, 9, 16
  and employability skills, 2, 3, 21–24,
    26, 27, 42, 45, 59–63, 70, 73, 77f,
    78–81
  negative aspects of, 52–54, 53t, 59,
    60, 64, 66, *see also* menial
    activities; punishment
  positive aspects of, 52–54, 53t, 60–61,
    64, 66, 67, 76–78, 77f, *see also*
    problem solving
  re-integrative benefits of, 2, 9, 11,
    16, 18, 25–26, 37, 40–46, 63–66,
    68–70, 76–78, 77f
  as requirement of CO, 16, 27n2,
    27n8
  stand alone, 16, 30, 35, 36–37t
  successful outcomes, measures for,
    76–78, 77f
  see also Community Payback;
    decorating; graffiti removal;
    'kindling preparation'; litter
    picking; menial activities;
    painting; shrub clearance

Varah, M., 3, 38t, 40, 41, 46, 52, 53t, 59,
    63, 66, 76, 77
vests of shame, 17, 27n11
Visible Unpaid Work Strategy
    (VUWS), 27n9

Warwickshire, 38t, 40
'what works' literature, 22–23, 26
Wilcox, A., 3, 20, 26, 30, 48t, 49–50,
    51t, 52, 53t, 54, 57–59
work placements, 2, 8, 17, 24, 48t,
    49–52, 53t, 55n2
  non skills-based/unskilled, 5, 40, 49,
    50, 52, 59t, 60, 64, 66–68, 70, 72
  offenders' attitudes to, 39t 41–42, 41t,
    49, 52, 59–63, 61t, 64, 67, 70–74
  skills-based, 41–42, 44, 45, 59t,
    60–61, 64, 71, 72–73, 76–78, 77f
  supervisors' opinion of, 61–63,
    65–66, 67–68, 69, 71, 73, 80
  see also unpaid work
Worrall, A., 8–10, 12, 25, 76, 79

young offender(s)
  attitudes toward re-offending,
    72–74
  and community benefits, 68–70
  community reparation's impact on,
    47–52, 59–66, 68–71
  'first-tier' disposals given to, 15, 18
  killing of James Bulger, 11–12
  and problem solving activities,
    63–66, 64t
  and punishment, 11, 66–68
  reconviction rates in, 46–47, 47t
  re-integrative intervention for,
    see youth justice community
    reparation (YJCR)
  response to work placements, 59–63,
    61t, 64, 67
  see also Youth Offending Team
    (YOT)
youth crime, 11–12, 13
Youth Crime Action Plan, 4, 54, 78
youth justice
  policy, 4, 14
  Reparation Order, 30, 44, 46–47
  'restorative' programmes, 20–21
  sanctions, 3, 49, 54
  system, 13, 14
  see also youth justice community
    reparation (YJCR)

DOI: 10.1057/9781137400468.0011

Youth Justice Board (YJB), 2, 4, 14, 15, 18, 20, 26–27, 30, 48t, 49, 54, 58, 63, 78, 79, 81

youth justice community reparation (YJCR)
  delivery in practice, 78–80
  evaluation of, 3–4
  implications for practice, 80–82
  introduction of, 11, 15, 25–26, 76
  limitations and future research implications, 82
  positive and negative practices in unpaid work, 52–54, 53t, 59
  post 2000, 16–21
  rebranding of, 18, see also '*Making Good*'
  reconviction results, 46–47, 47t
  studies into, 47–52, *see also* studies into YJCR
  see also Youth Offending Team (YOT)

Youth Justice Criminal Evidence Act (YJCA) (1999), 14

Youth Offending Service (YOS), 14

Youth Offending Team (YOT), 3, 4–6, 6n2, 18, 27n2, 46, 54
  acquisition of employability skills, 59–63, 61t
  assessment of the pilot, 48t, 49
  budget allocation to, 63, 69, 81–82
  case files, secondary data, 57–58, 57f, 58f
  and community benefits, 68–70
  inadequacies of, 59–63, *see also* menial activities; punishment
  'local' evaluation of projects, 48t, 51, 52
  members of, 14
  problem solving activities, 63–66
  punishment of offenders, 66–68
  re-offending attitudes of offenders, 72–74
  and reparation by offenders, 70–71

Youth Rehabilitation Order (YRO), 18, 26, 27n2, 30

CPSIA information can be obtained
at www.ICGtesting.com
Printed in the USA
LVOW12*1001110516

487732LV00007B/30/P